NEITHER TRUMPETS
NOR
VIOLINS

Also by Theodore Dalrymple from
New English Review Press:

Anything Goes (2011)

Farewell Fear (2012)

Threats of Pain and Ruin (2014)

Out into the Beautiful World (2015)

The Proper Procedure and Other Stories (2017)

Grief anf Other Stories (2018)

The Terror of Existence: From Ecclesiastes to Theatre of the Absurd (with Kenneth Francis) (2018)

NEITHER TRUMPETS

NOR

VIOLINS

**Philosophic reflections by
Theodore Dalrymple, Samuel Hux,
& Kenneth Francis**

Published by New English Review Press
a subsidiary of World Encounter Institute
PO Box 158397
Nashville, Tennessee 37215
&
27 Old Gloucester Street
London, England, WC1N 3AX

Cover design by Kendra Mallock
Cover art: *Vanitas with Violin and Glass Ball* by Pieter Claesz

ISBN: 978-1-943003-56-3

First Edition

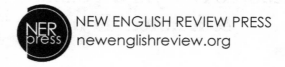

NEW ENGLISH REVIEW PRESS
newenglishreview.org

"[A] well stocked mind is safe from boredom."
—Arthur C. Clarke, *Childhood's End.*

Contents

FRIEDRICH NIETZSCHE (1844-1900)

THEODORE DALRYMPLE

W E LIVE IN A Nietzschean age, at least in the sense that the drive for power often seems to be the main motivation of people's behaviour, now more than ever. Of course, there have always been people who sought power, usually at the apex of society: but the desire for power, and the consequent struggle for it, seems to have filtered down and reached almost every stratum. It is as though power were the only desideratum, being to human conduct what the gold standard once was to a currency. Power alone stands guarantee that we shall not be trampled into the dust; all other protections are illusory, being but fig leaves for the power of others by which they disguise their prepotency from us.

People who might once have been content to serve, either in a personal or collective capacity, now find their powerlessness to be a humiliation. Subordination within a hierarchy is felt as a wound, an insult to the ego, and therefore accepted with an ill grace, if at all. This is visible in small matters: those who are required to wear a uniform take a pride in not wearing it with pride, and often subvert its intention by little acts of rebellion, such as a tie loosened at the collar, the wearing of shoes that are conspicuously ill-assorted with the rest of the outfit, and so forth. One must at all costs be an individual, and how can one be an individual if one is subordinate to others and do precisely what is demanded of one?

The inflamed need for individuation might thus be interpreted as a manifestation of the drive for power: for how can one exert power, or for that matter resist it, without being an individual? The relatively swift spread of tattooing and other forms of self-mutilation in Western society, even among classes and the type of people that would once have scorned them, is a symptom of a desperate need to mark oneself out, in the most literal sense, from others. As Freud said (falsely) that dreams were the royal road to the unconscious, so many people behave as if they believed (with equal lack of truth) that a tattoo is the royal road to individuation. It is not easy, after all, to stand out as one in seven billion, the current population of the world, all the more so as increasingly the seven billion live in huge agglomerations in which it is all too easy to feel about as individual as an ant in an anthill, and certainly one is often treated as such. Perhaps, then, it is not surprising that struggles for power now unsettle all hierarchies, no matter how insignificant they themselves may be by comparison with other hierarchies or with society as a whole, or that efforts at individuation should take morbid or antinomian forms.

Nietzsche, as has often been remarked, was not the kind of philosopher—if philosopher in any real sense he was at all, which some have denied[1]—who propounded a more or less

---

1 It is undeniable that Nietzsche has had a great influence, not among techni-

clear doctrine, to be accepted or rejected, modified or refined. He created, rather, a climate of opinion, as Auden put it with regard to Freud; and it is not a climate that I, for one, find very congenial. Of course, a Nietzschean might retort that Nietzsche was not put on earth to bring comfort to persons such as I, rather the reverse. Nietzsche himself, to whom grandiosity was far from alien, might reply, with Jesus, *Think not that I am come to send peace on earth: I came not to send peace, but a sword.*

In so far as a coherent philosophy can be attributed to Nietzsche, it is in his attempt to deal with the existential situation of Man once God was dead for him, and the meaninglessness of life consequent, or supposedly consequent, upon that demise. He then tried to find or attach a meaning to the life of Man, or at least of men.

Thus Nietzsche starts from an historical or sociological *aperçu*, namely that religious belief in the West is dead, or so moribund that it is inevitably destined for death. This *aperçu* can be contested, for however weakened religious belief may be, it persists to some degree and may one day revive. But I think that Nietzsche is here in essence right, irrespective of whether the arguments for or against the existence of God are valid. The long, melancholy withdrawing roar that Matthew Arnold heard on Dover beach is now more or less complete. Not God, but religion is dead as an intellectual force in Western life, and is unlikely to revive, soon at least: and in the last analysis, it is ideas that count.

It is a symptom of Nietzsche's grandiosity, to me somewhat pathetic and possibly a symptom of his incipient General Paralysis of the Insane, the last stage of neurosyphilis, that he should have thought himself as original and unprecedented a thinker as he did think himself.[2] His statement, "That a psycholo-

---

cal philosophers, but among people of literary and artistic culture. Thus Bertrand Russell, in *History of Western Philosophy,* Allen and Unwin, 1946, p. 794.

2 To analyse a statement or philosophy not according to its truth but according, as a matter of philosophic principle, to its origins is, in my opinion, to enter a hellish downward spiral of *ad hominem* name-calling: but there is a delicious, or malicious, irony in doing precisely this to the ideas of Nietzsche, attributing them to his neurosyphilis. He, after all, insisted more than most on

gist without equal speaks from my writings, is perhaps the first insight reached by a good reader,"[3] is boastful to the point of madness. He was a good psychologist of the intuitive kind, but the first insight reached by a good reader who was also a doctor might be that he was suffering from *folie de grandeur* when he wrote this assertion.

His atheism was by no means original or unprecedented, and in fact he provided no new philosophical argument in its favour. He accepted atheistic arguments without adding to them; he was more concerned with the consequences, psychological and sociological, than with the truth or otherwise of the atheistic position. On the question of the existence of God, he was not a philosopher at all.

According to Nietzsche, Man was all alone in a vast and meaningless universe that existed for nothing that resembled a purpose, but again he was far from the first to apprehend this. One has only to think of Macbeth's famous speech to realise this:

> Tomorrow, and tomorrow, and tomorrow,
> Creeps in this petty pace from day to day,
> To the last syllable of recorded time;

---

examining the psychological or morbid origins of philosophical ideas, and deciding on their worth—generally nil—on those grounds. "The grandiose form [of GPI]... is less common than simple dementia. Patients of this type are euphoric and develop delusions in which they figure as exceptional persons endowed with superhuman strength... or other magnificent attributes... and they see no discrepancy between their imaginary attributes and their debilitated and unfortunate actual condition. Other emotional states may dominate the picture, leading to so-called depressed, agitated, maniacal, and circular types.... As the patient becomes worse, however, the symptoms of dementia become more prominent, and in the terminal stage there is little evidence of any mental activity..." Russell Brain, *Diseases of the Nervous System*, 4th edition, Oxford University Press, 1951, pp. 428-9. This fits Nietzsche's case almost exactly. He was undoubtedly a brilliant man to start with, but professors of classical philology rarely end up by writing books starting with a section on "why I am so clever." The only case of GPI I ever saw in my career—for the disease had by then been almost eradicated by penicillin—was in a clergyman, which no doubt would have delighted Nietzsche.

3 *Ecce Homo*

And all our yesterdays have lighted fools
The way to dusty death. Out, out, brief candle!
Life's but a walking shadow, a poor player,
That struts and frets his hour upon the stage,
And then is heard no more. It is a tale
Told by an idiot, full of sound and fury,
Signifying nothing.

Of course, Shakespeare is the author *par excellence* who, thanks to his ability to enter the worlds of others, is not to be identified with his characters: we cannot deduce from Macbeth's words that Shakespeare thought that life signified nothing. But it seems to me unlikely that he would not have known, or intuited, what at least it was *like* to feel as Macbeth felt. Even if Shakespeare were a believer in God, we may surmise that he had had his doubts; but whether or not he had actually had them, he gave to Macbeth words that encapsulated the existential nihilism that Nietzsche foresaw as a mass phenomenon in the near future, at least of Europe.

Was Nietzsche right in his apprehension of the consequences of the mass loss of religious faith? Given the vast number of variables in the history of a civilization as complex as that of Europe, it is unlikely that any answer could be given that would compel consent from all reasonable persons. Certainly, contemplating the century after Nietzsche's death, no one could deny that that his prediction that there would be bloody wars and upheavals has been borne out. But was the loss of religious faith either a necessary or a sufficient condition for these disastrous events? The Thirty Years' War must give us pause; and if someone were to claim that religious differences were only the pretext, not the *real* cause of that war in which a third of the German population perished, it would still be the case that the leaders of, and participants in, that general conflagration were believers, and that their faith did nothing to prevent or even moderate it.

It is certainly true, however, that the mass killings of the twentieth century, both in international and civil wars or conflicts, were pursued in the name of general and transcendent ideas and ends. Freedom, nationalism, communism, social and economic justice, and racial purity, were (and still are) ideas that transcend the individual and can give to him an apparent purpose to life that is not merely personal. But nationalism and religious belief were not incompatible.

Nietzsche foresaw the importance, indeed the necessity, of human transcendence in a universe deprived of intrinsic meaning or purpose. Where could it come from? Mankind would have to find it for, and in, itself. There was also the problem of the moral law. If there were no God and no providential or teleological meaning to the Universe, upon what could moral principles or judgments be based? What was their ground?

Of course, for atheists, even the existence of God would not solve the problem: for supposing that the will of God could be known, and that there were some indubitable method—to use managerialist language—of accessing it, that is to say to know His intentions beyond all doubt, there would remain the problem of whether God Himself was good. In other words, the logical problem of the foundation of moral judgment precedes that of the existence of God. If we say that we obey God because He is good, our notion of the good precedes and is independent of that of God; if, on the other hand, we say that what God wishes is the definition of the good, we have in effect abdicated all moral judgment. We are simply following God because He is all-powerful, and to go against the all-powerful would be foolish, even if it were possible.

To this a believer might reply that we know God is good because the universe and life, indeed existence itself, is good; but not only is this a judgment that is not compelled by the evidence, at least not for everyone, and there have been many who would deny or have denied it, but even this assertion demands a capacity to judge good and ill antecedent to what is to be judged. If existence itself is deemed good, it could also be deemed bad: to die is good, said Solon, but never to have been born is best. And all this is quite separate from the problem in any case of knowing what God, if He existed, actually decreed for us. How do we know what He wants or demands of us? No doubt fundamentalists who believe in some text or other as the direct word of God would claim that it could be known; but such texts are often in languages which the believers do not speak, whose translations are uncertain, and whose meanings are disputable, even by people who believe that they are the direct word of God. As there is no honour among thieves, so there is no agreement among fundamentalists, as wars of religion sufficiently prove.

Nietzsche, then, set out to solve what he thought were the existential problems facing Mankind, at least in Europe, namely those of the purpose of life and the principles by which life should be guided or led. With the increasing realisation that God was dead—dead for Mankind, that is, for of course an atheist maintains that He never existed independent of Mankind, who manufactured Him for its own needs and purposes—the problems would grow only more acute and all-engrossing. Perhaps he cannot be blamed for not having solved them, since as far as I am aware no one else has done so either, at least not in the sense that the solution compels the assent of all reasonable people, but I personally find the scorn he pours on others who have tried, and his tendency to self-praise, distinctly uncongenial.

That Mankind must make judgments even without a moral or aesthetic Archimedean point from which to lever them is demanded by life itself. One cannot escape the necessity to judge, as Nietzsche recognised, even if one can avoid censoriousness (with which judgment is often confused, usually by those who want to avoid a prohibition or grant themselves permission to do something previously forbidden). Life has its obligations which cannot be avoided, even if they can sometimes be evaded.

Four aspects of Nietzsche are indissolubly associated with his name in most people's minds, at least of those who have ever considered him at all: his appropriation by the Nazis as their favourite philosopher, his notion of the will to power, his transvaluation (or overturning) of all values, and his ferocious hatred of Christianity.[4]

---

4 His doctrine of the eternal return, enunciated in *Thus Spake Zarathustra*, according to which everything that happens, has happened and will happen,

To take his appropriation by the Nazis first: it was neither justified nor completely incomprehensible. The keeper of the Nietzschean flame after his mental collapse was his sister, Elisabeth Förster-Nietzsche, who was a ferocious nationalist and anti-Semite. There is a famous photograph of her being visited at home by Hitler, her face wreathed with an expression of fatuous senile beatitude, Hitler bowing almost with deference towards her as the honoured bearer of the flame.

But Nietzsche was not a German nationalist and had many disobliging things to say about Germany and the Germans, particularly in their Wilhelmine incarnations, which he regarded as lumpen, vulgar, crude and uncultivated. Nor was he an anti-Semite, if he was not always philo-Semitic either, and indeed despised anti-Semitism.[5] Had he survived until 1933, or to the ascent of Nazism, he would have been so anti-Nazi that he would have had to retreat to Switzerland (of which country he remained a citizen for most of his life). To take but one passage from *Beyond Good and Evil*:

> Owing to the pathological estrangement which the insanity of nationality has induced, and still induces, among the peoples of Europe; owing also to the short-sighted and quick-handed

---

will be repeated an infinite number of times, seems to me mad, and metaphysical to an absurd degree. I do not think that it has had much influence, either practically or in theory.

5 Ambiguity is evident in a letter that he wrote to either his mother or his sister about the translator into English of *Beyond Good and Evil*. "I had the privilege," he wrote, "of introducing this 'champion of women's rights' [Fraulein von Salis] to another 'champion' who is my neighbour at meals, Miss Helen Zimmern, who is extremely clever, incidentally not an Englishwoman—but Jewish. May heaven have mercy on the European intellect if one wanted to subtract the Jewish intellect from it." The latter compliment might easily be turned against Jews once the paranoid stance towards them takes hold of a mind, for intelligence is not virtue in those believed to be evilly-disposed, rather the reverse; moreover, there is in the phrase "incidentally not an Englishwoman—but Jewish" an implicit belief that Jews cannot be citizens of a nation *simpliciter*. In *The Case of Wagner*, a late work, Nietzsche implies in a footnote that the manifold defects of the man and composer might be attributable to the fact that he was not really a German at all, despite his nationalism: surely a code for him having been of Jewish origin.

politicians who are at the top today with the help of this insanity, without any inkling that their separatist policies can of necessity only be *entr'acte* policies; owing to all this and much else that today simply cannot be said, the most unequivocal portents are now being overlooked, or arbitrarily and mendaciously reinterpreted—that *Europe wants to become one.*

Whatever you may think of this as prognostication, whatever inexactitudes it may contain and difficulties it skates over without noticing them, this sounds much more like a paean of praise to the European Union than an adherence to the philosophy (if that is quite the word for it) of Nazism.

At the same time, he wrote things that, if isolated from the rest of his work, would certainly give aid and comfort to Nazism, or any completely unscrupulous movement like it. His very style, though much praised, seems to me at any rate, who can read him only in English, rather like ranting. Opening *Beyond Good and Evil* at random, my eyes alight on the following:

> Nobody is very likely to consider a doctrine true merely because it makes people happy or virtuous—except perhaps the lovely 'idealists' who become effusive about the good, the true, and the beautiful and allow all kinds of motley, clumsy, and benevolent desiderata to swim around in utter confusion in their pond.

This is good knock-about fun, perhaps, but it breathes contempt for those of a different view, and there is undoubtedly a lot of spleen in his writing, which gets in the way of good judgment:

> They are no philosophical race, these Englishmen: Bacon signified an *attack* on the philosophical spirit; Hobbes, Hume and Locke a debasement and lowering of the value of the concept of 'philosophy' for more than a century. It was against that Kant arose, and rose; it was Locke of whom Schelling said, *understandably, 'je méprise Locke'*; in their fight against the English-mechanistic doltification of the world, Hegel and

Schopenhauer were of one mind...[6]

He continues two paragraphs later:

> It is characteristic of such an unphilosophical race that it clings firmly to Christianity.

But whatever you may think of Hume or John Stuart Mill as philosophers, to say nothing of Gibbon as a philosophical historian, they can hardly be accused of clinging firmly, or indeed at all, to Christianity. And if Nietzsche's animadversion is meant to apply to the people more than to the philosophers, it would have to be shown that the English clung more to Christianity than, say, the Germans, which might be difficult; and even then, it would also have to be shown that they did so *because* they were unphilosophical. Christianity, after all, has not been entirely without its philosophers—unless it be claimed that, *by definition*, no Christian can be a philosopher and no philosopher a Christian, in which case what Nietzsche says is merely a tautology.

The evident contradiction within so short a space is by no means uncharacteristic of a man who habitually lets his irritation get the better of his expression of even a partial truth.

There are passages in Nietzsche on which it is impossible to place anything but a deeply unpleasant construction, to put it mildly, as for example when he claims that a single heroic figure would justify the sufferings of untold numbers of people who came before him. Nietzsche states the following:

> The [French] Revolution made Napoleon possible: that is its justification. For the sake of a similar prize one would have to desire the anarchic collapse of our entire civilization...the value of a human being... does not reside in his usefulness: for it would continue to exist even if there were nobody to whom he could be useful. And why could the human being

---

6 It is surely odd that Kant should have been awakened from his dogmatic slumbers, as he called them, by a mere dolt, as he said he was awakened by Hume.

from whom the most deleterious effects have resulted not be the summit of the entire species man: so elevated, so superior that everything perished from envy of him?[7]

On this view of the matter, one would say, if one were a Nazi, that the slaughter of the First World War was justified by the advent of Hitler or, if one were a democrat, that Nazism was justified by the establishment of the Federal Republic of Germany, the most scrupulously democratic state in all German history. Causal historical links are not, and cannot be, justifications after the fact, however; nevertheless, as we shall see, Nietzsche thought that unintended consequences redounded to the credit of whatever caused them.

It seems to me to be obvious that the quotation above is not very far, at least in its atmosphere of ruthlessness, from Nazi barbarity; it is not altogether different in sensibility from Himmler's infamous speech to the S.S. extolling their hardness, as if their very ruthlessness was some kind of guarantee of virtue. Nietzsche praised hardness and self-overcoming, and the S.S. were nothing if not hard and self-overcoming, as Himmler recognised.[8]

Nietzsche was undoubtedly a fine intuitive psychologist, as was La Rochefoucauld,[9] but like many other clever intellectuals, he was inclined to take a short cut to total explanations of exis-

---

7 This is an extract from *The Will to Power*, admittedly a posthumous compilation by his sister, Elisabeth Förster-Nietzsche, from his notes, which Nietzsche never saw through the press. But though his sister had an axe to grind, no one has ever suggested that she made up the passages that she published from his notes.

8 There is another similarity between Nietzsche and Himmler. Both men extolled physical vigour and strength, but strictly in theory, that is to say for others. For themselves, they were poor physical specimens. No doubt we are all inclined to extol and enviously identify with what we are not and cannot be. Not for nothing was Nietzsche a fine sniffer-out and dissector of *ressentiment*.

9 Compare, for example, La Rochefoucauld's remark that there is in the misfortune of our friends something not unpleasing, with Nietzsche's, that those who fight monsters should be careful not to become monsters themselves. They are of a similar penetration, being obvious and revelatory at the same time, and expressed with a similar compression.

tence or solutions of its problems. Marx, for example, saw economic interest as the key to human behaviour, and even made it, in his *Theses on Feuerbach*, an epistemological principle: people thought as it was in their economic interest to think. With Freud, of course, it was sex, and with Nietzsche it was power and the urge to increase it. The underlying explanation of all human conduct was thus economic interest, sex, or the search for power.

No one would deny that these things are important in human life, and in individuals one or other of them may be predominant. But this rather modest observation will excite, or even interest, no one.

We can take Marx's dictum that being determines consciousness, and not consciousness being, in one of two ways: either as a psycho-sociological generalisation, in which case it is true much of the time (we think most of the time as others in our historical and economic position think), but so obvious as hardly to excite comment; or as a law of thought, of universal application, governing all human cerebration whatever, in which case it is obviously false. One is reminded of what Doctor Johnson said to an aspiring author: your book is both true and original, but the parts which are true are not original, and the parts which are original are not true.

Nietzsche, by contrast, saw the will to power everywhere, as much in the person who helps lepers as in the one who slaughters multitudes. And it is certainly true that, for example, excessive generosity by a very wealthy person towards someone who has hardly a bean to his name can be, and is intended to be, humiliating. On the other hand, it can be a manifestation of benevolent generosity which is gratefully received or comes as a great relief and nothing else.

Pity can be condescending, no doubt, and we suspect persons who claim an excess of it to be humbugs, moral exhibitionists who are seeking attention and often power. Legion are the people who seek to do good at others' expense. But this should not prevent us from seeing that there are people who devote themselves to the relief of suffering from a good heart.

It is true that they often make us feel uncomfortable, because they seem better persons than ourselves, but the problem is with us, not with them. In the film of Che Guevara's motorcycle ride through South America, which apparently persuaded him of the necessity of later executing large numbers of people in Cuba, we see him arriving in a leper colony run by nuns, where he mixes freely and without constraint with the lepers in the kind of joyful, spontaneous way of which Nietzsche would have approved, unlike the dour nuns who keep aloof from the lepers to whom they extend but a cold charity, which Nietzsche would have interpreted as the expression of a drive, or lust for power. What is forgotten, of course, in these scenes is that Guevara soon rides away leaving the nuns and lepers behind. Moreover, very few of those who watched the film would have known that leprosy is a disease that is not contracted by casual contact, but by prolonged and intimate contact of the kind that nuns who looked after lepers for years might have been expected to have: therefore, even if the cold conduct of the nuns were a true portrayal, there would have been at least a partial excuse for it. In fact, I encountered nuns in Africa who devoted their lives to lepers and they were not at all as portrayed in the film (though, of course, times might have changed), and when I wrote a brief article in praise of them, I was surprised by the vehemence of the hatred, the venom, with which respondents to the article expressed themselves. I had not in the slightest endorsed the religious beliefs of the nuns, which I did not share, but without which I doubted that they would have behaved as selflessly as they did; instead, I merely reported on what seemed to me the charity of their conduct.

The replies were Nietzschean all. Nuns were not charitable but seekers after power. Those who had attended convent schools, or schools run by the Christian Brothers (a Catholic lay order), described the sadistic treatment that they had received. The nuns in Africa were power-hungry sadists who simply concealed their sadistic power-drive better: but it was there, all right, *ex officio*.

Seeing power-seeking in benevolence as a matter of principle is like the denial of the possibility of altruism because altruism brings satisfaction to the person who is altruistic, directly or indirectly, for example by satisfying him that he has done his duty, thus giving rise to the sin of pride. This, however, tells us nothing about the world or human conduct because it is true by definition, that is to say a tautology. It is simplistic and allows no possibility of the admixture of motives. I may derive satisfaction from performing a good deed, but that does not mean that I do not genuinely wish the person well for whom I have performed the deed. Surgeons work for money, but that does not mean that they do not care whether or not they save their patients' lives provided they are paid (or accorded social respect, etc.).

According to Nietzsche, expressions of pity for the suffering, whether in word or deed, are the means by which the powerless and the resentful seek revenge for their own situation and the power that will assuage it. There is undoubtedly a grain of truth here, but a grain does not make a loaf of bread. No doubt it was an acute intuition of Nietzsche's that supposed sympathy for or outrage at the sufferings of others, real or imagined or both, might be a useful lever to power, and furthermore that the danger of this being done was becoming ever greater. But it is surely not the case that every expression of pity is merely disguised resentment, a search for power and revenge on the formerly powerful. It is true that Nietzsche would at once have seen through Lenin's supposed desire to improve the condition of humanity, but he was far from the only one who would have been, or was, able to do so,[10] nor was any great philosophical apparatus necessary to do so.

In fact, Adam Smith (who would be regarded by most people as a cynic because of his belief in the invisible hand) seems to me to be very much closer to the general truth than Nietzsche ever came:

How selfish soever man may be supposed, there are evidently

---

10   Bertrand Russell, whose style of philosophy Nietzsche would certainly have despised, was able to do so. See his *The Practice and Theory of Bolshevism*, 1920.

some principles in his nature, which interest him in the fortune of others, and render their happiness necessary to him,
though he derives nothing from it except the pleasure of seeing it.[11]

Smith goes on to say, with equal realism in my view, that
there is also a similar principle that makes us sympathise with
the suffering of others and wish to relieve it. Clearly there are
exceptions, and these are not invariable rules or laws of human
psychology, but fortunately are closer to my experience of life
than Nietzsche's preferred world. The book by the anthropologist, Colin Turnbull, about an African tribe, the Ik, in whom
circumstances had encouraged a complete lack of either sympathy or empathy of one person for another, even of a parent
for his or her child, describes a world that is Nietzschean to the
last degree, and is a world in which sooner or later a superman might be expected to emerge: though only a psychopath,
self-confident in his ruthlessness, would be attracted to it.[12]

Nietzsche would have despised Smith's ideas, which he
would have found shallow (as indeed they would have been,
if they had been intended as universal laws of human thought
and conduct rather than rough generalisations) and even their
cool and detached mode of expression, though passion is not
obviously a condition of the truth of words. But Nietzsche, if he
had cared to, could have acknowledged their truth, including of
himself, as the famous incident when he embraced an ill-used
and suffering horse demonstrates. Perhaps the truth is not very
interesting, sometimes because we all know it already, but it is
still the truth.

Nietzsche was a practitioner of what Paul Ricœur called *the
hermeneutics of suspicion*. Freud and Marx were other practitioners, though even Freud said that sometimes a cigar was just
a cigar: though, to practice the hermeneutics of suspicion, he

---

11 Adam Smith, *The Theory of Moral Sentiments*, 1759.

12 Colin Turnbull, *The Mountain People*, Simon & Schuster, 1972. Turnbull's
account has been criticised as grossly inaccurate, but at the very least it is interesting as a thought experiment.

might have chosen this example because he liked cigars. At any rate, Freud thought it took himself to be able to discern when a cigar was just a cigar, and when it was 'really' something else. According to the hermeneutics of suspicion, what I really mean, when I say to someone, "Good morning" with a cheerful expression, is "Go to the devil!"

It is surely no discovery that words (as well as actions) often have more than a literal meaning.[13] In a sense, then, we all practise the hermeneutics of suspicion, even if we are not aware that that is what we are doing. Only a child or a simpleton takes every word at its literal meaning. But disguise would not be successful, perhaps not even possible, and would certainly fail in its intention, if there were no literal truthfulness and nothing but disguise. Disguise is parasitic on truth.

When Nietzsche tells us that there are no facts, only interpretations (at the service of the will to power), is that itself a fact? Nietzsche in his arguments often appeals to facts: like Marx, then, he exempts himself, god-like, from his own epistemology. Somehow, Marx escaped in his thoughts and doctrines from his own position as a member of the bourgeoisie, and Nietzsche escaped from the impossibility of factual knowledge to show that in fact there were no facts.

It is often said in defence of Nietzsche that what he wrote did not mean what it appears to mean on first reading, that in fact it means something very different, and much subtler. Thus, when he says, "The great epochs of our life come when we gain the courage to rechristen our evil as what is best in us,"[14] this is not to give *carte blanche* to our worst impulses. But it is noteworthy that Nietzsche does not qualify the statement by adding "sometimes" or "often," which might make it sometimes contain an element of truth; and he is to be blamed if people con-

---

13 A delightful little book was published in the 1950s in the series *Que sais-je?* of the Presses Universitaires de France, titled *La Vie Anglaise*. Here it was explained that, in the middle-class England of the time, an expression such as "How lovely to see you, we must meet again soon" actually means, "What a bore, under no circumstances do I ever want to meet you again."

14 *Beyond Good and Evil.*

clude from his statement that, say, their inclination to ill-temper should be given full rein. A writer is not fully responsible, perhaps, for what people make of his writings, but he is not entirely lacking in responsibility for it either. Were Nietzsche's thoughts really so vastly complex and subtle that they could not be given unequivocal, or at any rate less equivocal, expression?

Let us take two examples, one good and one bad, from the same source. First the good:

> When we have to change our minds about a person, we hold the inconvenience he causes us very much against him.

This is acute in precisely the way that La Rochefoucauld is acute; one recognises its truth at once.

But now let us take another dictum:

> Even concubinage has been corrupted—by marriage.

Here, it seems to me, Nietzsche prefers a statement that shocks to one that is true, perhaps because one that was true on this subject would be something that everyone knows and that would be so hedged around with qualifications that it would be boring both to enunciate and to read. In this sense, Nietzsche has an attitude towards truth that reminds one of that of George Bernard Shaw, who often preferred a good *bon mot* to a dull truism: the difference being that Shaw was more obviously a seeker of celebrity, including notoriety, than Nietzsche. On the subject of marriage, it would be true to say that a bad one is hell, a good one is bliss, and that there are marriages of every grade in between. Moreover, some marriages are corrupt, abusive, and so forth, but some are loving, mutually supportive, and so forth: but we don't really need to be told this.

If the object of a philosopher is more than merely to seek truth and express it as best he can, but rather to have some social effect, for example rattling the tin box of human complacency, he cannot be absolved of responsibility for the effect that he actually *does* have, irrespective of his intentions. And I find it difficult to think of any good that has come of infatuation with Nietzsche.[15]

Of course, going against the grain, or swimming against the tide, may be, and often is, of service, but only if it is done in the name of truth. When Nietzsche tells us in *The Case of Wagner* that "morality negates life," he cannot, does not, mean that there is no good and bad. He speaks at the same time of the good and evil in Wagner: "Once one has developed a keen eye for the symptoms of decline, one understands morality, too—one understands what is hiding under its most sacred names and value formulas: impoverished life..."

Decline, impoverished life: these are terms of moral judgment. But for myself, I cannot see that his Dionysian fantasies, elaborated at the *tables d'hôte* and guest houses of Switzerland and Italy, represent an improvement: on the contrary, they may have contributed to the downward spiral that he saw with considerable acuity, and which accounts for his continuing popularity. To be free of humanitarian restraint: what a relief, especially for print-ridden intellectuals!

---

15 Both Michel Foucault and Ayn Rand were followers. I suspect that they excoriated philanthropic sentiments because they were incapable of feeling any themselves. Nietzsche would thus appeal to them.

Trumbull Stickney

"SIR, SAY NO MORE:"
DEMOTING WITTGENSTEIN,
MOURNING TRUMBULL STICKNEY

SAMUEL HUX

I AM TONE-DEAF TO Ludwig Wittgenstein. I'm not proud of that fact—but I'm not embarrassed either. I am *almost* tone-deaf to Mozart, and I am embarrassed to admit it. I know at some necessary level (because I am not an idiot) that he is superior to Jean Sibelius, but I would rather listen to the Finnish master any day. I cannot think at the moment of any philosopher I would not prefer reading to Wittgenstein, whether one as lucid as I find William James or as beating-my-head-against-the-wall as I experience Immanuel Kant—so I am not tone-deaf to Wittgenstein because he is too difficult, but because . . . well, because I find his relative lucidity *barren*.

27

It may be that I've spent so much time discussing and lecturing on Plato, Aristotle, Augustine, Descartes, and James (to name but a few I delight in), who tackle what I take to be the great problems of Western philosophy, that I find Wittgenstein so prickly and niggling, but I cannot be proud of the fact that I cannot follow my betters such as Bertrand Russell in discovering what made his colleague Ludwig so wonderful. Not that Ludwig appreciated Bertie's appreciation. When the *Tractatus Logico-Philosophicus* (1921) was published in English in 1922, by Russell's intervention, Wittgenstein was angry at Russell for his introduction, claiming Russell did not understand the work. If Russell did not understand Wittgenstein, who does? Certainly not I. Nor, I suspect, do his enthusiasts, much less those who think him the greatest philosopher of the twentieth century. I should emend that last sentence: they do not understand the significance of the fact that Wittgenstein is so celebrated—which judgment, however, gets me ahead of myself.

I remember being stunned several years ago by the realization that I had heard more classical concerts than had Mozart. I hear not only what's played in concert halls but on the seldom silent radio in home or auto; Mozart, without my technological advantage, could hear only what was played in his presence. Here's a relevant analogy: I have read more classical philosophy than Ludwig Wittgenstein. A philosophy major or minor at a respectable college or university (before at least the "relevance" revolution in higher education) has read more. Wittgenstein, finding the classical tradition of Western philosophy even into the twentieth century a large mistake, read relatively little of what he found mistaken. (This fact did not really make him an eccentric in Oxbridgean philosophical circles. Bryan Magee in his memoir, *Confessions of a Philosopher,* recalled how there were extraordinary gaps in the philosophical curriculum at Oxford when he was a student, great swathes of thought, Kant for instance, foreign to the anti-metaphysical bias of logical positivism and other forms of British-style "analytic philosophy.")

While tone-deaf to Wittgenstein as I've confessed, I am not resistant to his (very) occasional charm. His favorite actress, according to his friend Norman Malcolm (*Ludwig Wittgenstein: A Memoir*), was the "Brazilian Bombshell" Carmen Miranda—which can be read as a total lack of taste, or, as I read it, a lovable bit of insanity. And then there is one of my favorite sentences in the philosophical literature, the first proposition of the *Tractatus*: "The world is all that is the case." First response: Well, what the hell else would it be? Then: Since "world" is not a geological designation, but all the somethings in coherent order, "The facts in logical space are the world,"—then what better way to say it than "The world is all that is the case?" Maybe there are better ways, but not more quirky-charming. But very quickly my patience with the *Tractatus* begins to recede.

I do not intend an analysis of, or another introduction to, Wittgenstein. (Should one need or want one, I know no better example of each than A.C. Grayling's *Wittgenstein: A Very Short Introduction*, in the Oxford University Press short introduction series, for its readability—especially given a subject that defies the adjective *readable*—and given the absence of hero worship, by which I mean Grayling considers the possibility that Wittgenstein may be, instead of a great philosopher, "one of the great personalities of philosophy.") I intend, as is already obvious, to lodge a kind of complaint, and incidentally a wonderment at the worshipful attitude of the academic profession I have myself professed—not very mainstream, I realize.

As I recall my undergraduate days at the University of North Carolina, before its philosophy department became, as I assume it did, an American island of British philosophical instruction, when it was instead a home to "Continental" philosophical biases, I have loving memories of being introduced to questions such as the nature of existence, of the soul, the limits of knowledge, the possibilities of choice, ethical standards, God or his absence, what beauty is, and-and-and the mystery of what lies beyond-behind perceivable physical reality . . . and the necessity of *talking about these matters*. But if I am to believe Wittgenstein, all these matters and all talk about these matters that changed my young life were merely the result of Western philosophy taking the wrong path because its practitioners did not grasp the nature of language; if philosophers made the nature of language their focus then the old questions which engaged my young mind would be shown to be spurious and would disappear. (Not quite incidentally, Martin Heidegger's prejudice—that word intended!—that philosophy took the wrong path with Plato accounts in large for my inability to engage fully with another candidate for "greatest philosopher of the century.")

Granted, there were modifications of the views Wittgenstein expressed in the *Tractatus*, those modifications appearing in his later work, most famously in *Philosophical Investigations*, but the "linguistic" emphasis remains, and the extraordinary reputation of Wittgenstein had set like concrete long before there were any modifications.

In any case: the clear message of the *Tractatus*, so exciting to a certain kind of philosopher, was anti-metaphysical. (Forget all the exacting particulars of the argument which are not my immediate concern here, and are available to any reader wishing to tackle the *Tractatus* or to be instructed by, let's say, Grayling.) Hence the famous last proposition of the work; this proposition is preceded by the statement that "The correct method in philosophy would really be the following: to say nothing except what can be said, i.e., propositions of natural science [since metaphysical statements are of necessity nonsense]." So: "What we cannot speak about we must pass over in silence." *Wovon man nicht sprechen kann, darüber muss man schweigen.* Or in the most popular translation, "Whereof one cannot speak, thereof one must be silent."

Granted, Wittgenstein does not say that what I and others have thought to be the "great questions" do not exist, they simply cannot be spoken of. Ethics, for example, may exist and we may be ethical, but ethics cannot logically be talked about because they have nothing to do with the "world that is all that is the case." The same with theological matters, which may . . . etc. But I really do rebel at this *diktat*, this assertion that whereof we cannot speak . . . because as a matter of fact, we can! At least poor benighted Kant thought he could: *The Metaphysics of Morals*. Rudolf Otto had a lot to say about the ineffable: *The*

Idea of the Holy. Perhaps they would have been rendered mute had they tried to speak in the pure language of logic, *if p is q*, etc. —But thank God. . . .

Furthermore: since we can . . . isn't it really the case that Wittgenstein might have been more forthright had he pronounced a different *diktat: Wovon man nicht sprechen muss, darüber muss man schweigen?* Whereof one must not speak, thereof one must be silent. I am not at all convinced that the *Tractatus* proves *cannot*; and I suspect that Wittgenstein did indeed mean that metaphysical (and such) matters simply *must* not be spoken of. There are familiar stories (Grayling repeats some) of Wittgenstein's pleasure when some of his bright students ceased doing philosophy and took to manual jobs instead, working in a canning factory, for instance.

Let us be frank and not dance around the issue. What is this, the avoidance of all metaphysical talk that made up the grand tradition of Western philosophy, the avoidance thereby applauded by so much of the philosophical professoriate, but philosophical *suicide?* That's what I meant when I said earlier that I find Wittgenstein's relative lucidity "barren."

I would not be so tone-deaf to Ludwig Wittgenstein had he said something like this: There really are some things that cannot be put in words—what we mean by "ineffable" (in Wittgenstein's German *unaussprechlich*)—but the glory of philosophical endeavor is that although we cannot express certain things, we heroically try to. That's my belief, in any case. For instance, Kant made a basic distinction between *phenomena*, all that is accessible to the senses, and the *noumena*, the thing-in-itself (*das ding-an-sich*) which lies-is-resides-hides behind or beyond phenomena and is inaccessible to the human mind. Yet there is a basic hunger to know what it is and how it exists, to the extent that some thinkers have tried to imagine it: for instance, Arthur Schopenhauer, who bravely, and to my mind (although I am a "fan") totally unconvincingly, identifies it as the blind "will" found even in us, *der Wille*. Say what one might about Schopenhauer (incidentally dismissed by Wittgenstein for having "quite a crude mind"), who is probably more famous for his justification of physical suicide than anything else, he did not commit philosophical suicide.

Wittgenstein surely knew of Niels Bohr, a vastly greater physicist than Wittgenstein was a philosopher, but I am unaware of any commentary on Bohr's insistence that although the natural language of physics was mathematics, the only logical way to describe events in the sub-atomic universe of quantum mechanics, it was nonetheless the responsibility of the scientist to try to convey to the layman the nature of those events in the language of ordinary intellectual discourse. For instance (my example, not necessarily Bohr's), when, as mathematics tells us, an elementary particle in one "orbit" within an atom takes a "quantum leap" to another, it does not traverse the space between orbits, but rather is just "in" the first orbit and then "in" the second without "moving" from one to the other—which defies common sense or even the extraordinary sense of classical Newtonian physics—this movement which isn't movement but rather a kind of ceasing to be "here" and coming to be "there" without any ceasing and becoming having occurred at all. Yet, the only way to describe it—an incomprehensible-for-most mathematics aside—is in the language of ordinary discourse as a "leap."

I think the truth is that not only was Niels Bohr a better physicist than Ludwig Wittgenstein was a philosopher, he was a better philosopher. I am tempted to say, metaphorically, he was a *poet*.

Clever transition, because I want now to talk about a poet: one who comes to mind for multiple reasons. But whatever the occasion for my idly recalling or wanting to read Trumbull Stickney again, invariably at some point in the engagement Ludwig Wittgenstein would come to mind. Hence the rather unorthodox linking here of these two historically unrelated figures, whom I doubt have occupied anyone else's mind at the same time. At first, I assumed the reason was a matter of disparities: Wittgenstein's 62 years to Stickney's 30; the former's great fame, the latter's relative obscurity; the philosopher's overblown achievement (in my estimation), the poet's great promise cut off by death. These contrasts are meaningless of course, merely accidental. Gradually, I understood what was knocking at my mind for attention: Joseph Trumbull Stickney (1874-1904) tried to an extent that surpasses what all true poets attempt to a degree, to say *what cannot be said.*

You will not find Trumbull Stickney in the standard anthologies, neither the relevant ones of the several Norton Anthologies nor Columbia University Press's *The Top 500 Poems* edited by William Harmon, which includes such dim leading lights as Clement Clarke Moore, Charles Wolfe, William Allingham, William Henry Davies, and Gelett Burgess—all very familiar to at least five people in the world—while excluding (and in effect de-canonizing) the extraordinary Elinor Wylie, H.D. (Hilda Doolittle), Edna St. Vincent Millay, and Conrad Aiken. The exclusion of the first two betrays a hopeless lack of taste, that of the last two is an aesthetic and historical scandal. Stickney's absence places him in glorious company.

Actually Stickney was never canonized in the first place, although Edwin Arlington Robinson (the near equal of Robert Frost, if truth be told) said upon his death: "We could not afford to lose him." This was not mere payback for Stickney being the author in *The Harvard Monthly* of the first positive review of Robinson's poetry: a Robinson biographer makes it clear that the admiration was real. Edmund Wilson (the best American literary critic of the twentieth century, bar none) tried to revive his brief reputation in a 1940 essay in *The New Republic* and in his foreword to *The Poems of Trumbull Stickney,* edited by Amberys R. Whittle, in which Wilson suggested why Stickney had not caught on by then, 1966, noting that Stickney was a traditional formalist, "which will probably make [him] seem alien to those who, following the technique of William Carlos Williams, *compose what they call their poems in a kind of broken-up prose*" (italics mine). Indeed.

Since the reader cannot be required to know Whittle's 1974 *Trumbull Stickney* or the English poet Seán Haldane's far more entailed 1970 critical biography, *The Fright of Time* (the title a Stickney line), here's a quick look at Stickney's brief life.

Stickney was born in Geneva in 1874, while his father, a classics scholar and professor at Trinity College in Harford, Connecticut, was on extended leave in Europe—a very extended leave indeed, since the Stickney family—the parents, Trumbull, and three siblings—spent most of its time abroad in Switzerland, Italy, France, Germany, and England, as if it were a creation of Henry James. Trumbull, at seventeen in 1891, privately educated except for a couple of brief stints, entered Harvard. There, he ignored the newly instituted elective system and chose the more demanding older course requirements, including those in literature, philosophy, and foreign languages: beyond the modern ones, Latin, Greek, and even Sanskrit. (Much later, he with the Parisian professor Silvain Lévi would translate the *Bhagavad Gita!*) At Harvard, he was from his freshman year on a member of the editorial board of *The Harvard Monthly* (which was far from a typical student publication) where he began his poetry publishing career, and gained the admiration of a man not given to admiration, George Santayana. Upon graduation, he successfully pursued a doctorate at the Sorbonne, the first ever awarded an Englishman or American. While in Paris, he published back home his only non-posthumous book of poems, *Dramatic Verses* (1902). He also wrote two dissertations for the *doctorat ès lettres*, one written in Latin on an Italian subject, one in French on Greek poetry. With doctorate in hand, he returned to Harvard in 1903 to teach Greek. By the summer of 1904, he was suffering from a brain tumor, lost his sight; in October, he slipped into a coma and died.

It is not only for this reason that I find Trumbull Stickney *one of the most* heart-breaking of poets. John Keats was the most. But on the other hand, Keats at twenty-five had already fulfilled his great promise, for how much greater could the second best poet in English have become? Stickney was only close to realizing his promise. Of course, he had five years more than Keats. But weigh this fact: Robert Frost published his first book when almost forty years of age, and lived two years beyond his reading at the inauguration of John F. Kennedy. Frost was born three months before Stickney in 1874.

Odd that a life that meant so much to older gentlemen—like Santayana, who wrote movingly of Stickney in *The Middle Years* (volume II of his *Persons and Places*), and the historian, novelist, and autobiographical author of *The Education of Henry Adams*, whom he knew in Paris—odd that it should be so remote from fame. Stickney was also a favorite of his contemporaries at Harvard, who recalled him with great affection, such as the poets George Cabot "Bay" Lodge and William Vaughan Moody, who saw to the posthumous publication in 1905 of Stickney's then-available poems.

All who remembered him commented on his great sensitivity, cultural endowments, and exquisite taste in all the arts. Santayana called him "one of the three best educated persons I have known." Should one get the impression of a merely desk-bound presence in a library or studio, one should be corrected: Moody described him thusly: "a picture of radiant youth—very tall, a figure supple and graceful as a Greek runner's, a face of singular brightness," which squares with the memory of a younger friend in Paris, that Stickney was 6'4" and "much resembled a Greek god, in spite of his curious staring eyes." The recollections of this younger friend reveal Stickney as, beyond the picture of aesthete and handsome devil, an extraordinarily responsible friend.

Anglo-Irish baronet Shane Leslie (Sir John Randolph Leslie) was but sixteen and seventeen when he knew Stickney in 1903 in Paris. In three different memoirs, published in 1936, 1938, and 1966, Leslie recalled how Stickney took him, young and naïve, under his wing and not only became a kind of cultural guide but shepherded him away from that "Proustian world" in Paris, "a society of secret decadence" like "the Cities of the Plain" (Sodom and Gomorrah), "a whole section of life which was as clear of ladies as an ecclesiastical seminary." I mention this to counter an impression that might be left by Santayana, who remarked that a small student coterie at Harvard disliked Stickney because he called a sunset "gorgeous," thus seeming "too literary and ladylike." Good grief! Even sixty-three years later—injured veteran of World War I, diplomat, prolific man of letters, all-around man of the world, first cousin of Winston Churchill—Leslie's memories of Stickney are nothing less than a kind of retroactive hero worship. Stickney was in Leslie's judgment (although not in his diction) all that a man should be, which is the meaning of the German and Yiddish word *Mensch.* A Mensch indeed.

Stickney's poems collected in Whittle's edition cover roughly 300 pages. (A selection of fifty or so edited in 1968 by Seán Haldane and James Reeves, *Homage to Trumbull Stickney,* is harder to find.) The Whittle collection has lyrics (sonnets included), dramatic monologues, mini-dramas, long and short fragments of uncompleted verse plays, and an extraordinary array of other fragments, probably a tenth of the above having appeared neither in the 1902 *Dramatic Verses* nor the 1905 collection put together by Bay Lodge and Will Moody. Some of the pieces are "juvenilia" rather than mature work. None of it is dismissible. Although the American critic R.P. Blackmur did just that in 1933, to his eternal shame. Editors at Norton and Columbia U. Press should have listened to poets. Horace Gregory said, "As one turns the pages of Stickney's posthumous poems . . . one seems to stand in the unshaded presence of poetic genius." The editors' taste did not excel that of some poets themselves who compiled anthologies: Louis Untermeyer, Mark Van Doren, Allen Tate, Oscar Williams, W.H. Auden, and Conrad Aiken himself, who wrote that Stickney was "the natural link between [Emily] Dickinson and the twentieth century 'thing.'"

Among the pure lyrics (non-sonnets) is a sequence of poems, "Eride," of 138 stanzas, one reason it was never anthologized. To say that the sequence is uneven is true . . . and also irrelevant. It is a heart-stopping expression of love, or better yet, memory of a love, the fate of which the reader never really knows. Two quatrains will have to do.

> Brown eyes I say, yet say I blue.
> I think her mouth is a melody,
> Her bosom a petal sunned and new;
> Her hand is a passing sigh.

Blue eyes I say, yet somehow brown.
Her mouth is the verge of all repose;
Her breast is a smoothed-out viol tone;
Her hand is an early rose.

Well, two quatrains might do if they did not suggest, no
matter how beautiful, a poem conventionally romantic. (Stickney changed decisively the intended title, "A Romance"). It is
a painful sequence as well, as is indicated by another quatrain
later on:

You have no pity, none. You live
Impatient and unreconciled.
Nay, were you a mother, I believe
You never could well love your child.

Or another:

Sometimes I think we never met,--
'T had surely better been, to spare
This nervous wringing of regret,
This hope that tightens to despair.

Stickney keeps returning to his difficult beloved in poems
composed later than this sequence, poems, however, if they had
not been arranged correctly by Bay Lodge and Will Moody, one
might assume were natural parts of the "Eride" sequence.
    In the lyric "Once," for instance:

If once again before I die
I drank the laughter of her mouth
And quenched my fever utterly,
I say, and should it cost my youth,
'T were well! for I no more should wait
Hammering midnight on the doors of fate.

Should one wonder at the title of the sequence, "Eride?" It belongs to no language that I know of, nor any that biographers have guessed at (or seem even curious about in Whittle's case). It's neither in the French, German, Italian, Latin, Greek, nor Sanskrit that Stickney knew. But the verbal clue *Er-* certainly suggests *Eros*, and given the sense of the poems . . . There's another possibility, although I find it ambiguous. Is it the beloved's name? If so, it could be derived from *Eris*, as is the name *Eridé* (with accent). Since *Eridé* as a first name seems to function only in Lithuanian . . . no need to finish the sentence. (Or maybe there is: we shall see in time.) Since *Eris* is the Greek goddess of strife and discord, as Stickney would well know . . . what closer connection is there between love and strife, as the Sanskrit *Kama Sutra* calls sexual love "flowery combat?"

Here's my guess, although I'll not make a big conclusive deal of it. Stickney wants to say something of a specific love which is past, still present, and hopefully may return, with no real borders between past, present, and future, because love is not situated comfortably in time. Nor is love *just love*, for there are too many kinds, so many that we can't be sure what they have in common to justify their having one name. Love of parent (for and by), sibling, friend, intimately beloved, partner, to say nothing of locale or country or hopes or memories or some near stranger whose appeal we cannot fathom—to suggest a minor number of its forms which might be individually named. Love being so many things and so complicated and so impossible-to-capture in one word, and *Eros* and *Eris* being no better, why not make up a word to suggest something that really cannot be said? So: *Eride*. Perhaps a minor instance of trying to honor the ineffable in one word which isn't a word. More of this a bit later.

Of the completed lyrics in Stickney's oeuvre (none of the intended full-length plays were completed), there are in my judgment—aside from parts of "Eride"—four or five (I'm being conservative) which deserve permanent places in the history of poetry in English. Perhaps the best (this was Edmund Wilson's opinion also) is "Mnemosyne" (memory). I cannot help but to quote it in its entirety.

It's autumn in the country I remember.

How warm a wind blew here about the ways!
And shadows on the hillside lay to slumber
During the long sun-sweetened summer-days.

It's cold abroad the country I remember.

The swallows veering skimmed the golden grain
At midday with a wing aslant and limber;
And yellow cattle browsed upon the plain.
It's empty down the country I remember.

I had a sister lovely in my sight:
Her hair was dark, her eyes were very somber;
We sang together in the woods at night.

It's lonely in the country I remember.

The babble of our children fills my ears,
And on our hearth I stare the perished ember
To flames that show all starry thro' my tears.

It's dark about the country I remember.

These are the mountains where I lived. The path
Is slushed with cattle-tracks and fallen timber,
The stumps are twisted by the tempest's wrath.

But that I knew these places are my own,
I'd ask how came such wretchedness to cumber
The earth, and I to people it alone.

It rains across the country I remember.

(A similar fragment—"I hear a river thro' the valley wan-
der / Where water runs, the song alone remaining, / A rainbow

stands and summer passes under"—inspired John Hollander's best poem, "Variations on a Fragment by Trumbull Stickney," which is clearly an imitation of and homage to "Mnemosyne.")

As Edmund Wilson observed, not a "poetic" word in the poem, the plainest language with, I'd suggest, only ember sounding lyrical, but the impression overall of the great tradition of English formal lyricism—no "broken-up prose" of a certainty.

I am not as enamored of Stickney's sonnets as most of his loyalists, but some are startling. "Be still, The Hanging Gardens were a dream" has been his most famous (if that's the right word). One which always startles me does so primarily not because of its total effect (as in "Mnemosyne") or its dramatic content, but because of images that could hardly be imagined and never expected. Beginning "Live blindly and upon the hour. The Lord, / Who was the Future, died full long ago," and moving toward an embrace of Greek paganism—"Thou art divine, thou livest, —as of old / Apollo springing naked to the light"—and concluding with an unforgettable image, "And all his island *shivered into flowers*" (italics mine). Stickney took his turn to a kind of Greek *Weltanschauung* seriously, by the way. He thought Plato's *Republic*, he wrote in a letter to his sister Lucy, "that greatest book of the human mind."

A long lyric, far too long for reproduction in an essay—it's 108 lines of irregular length, rhyming but in nothing suggesting a pattern, so a different formalism than that of "Mnemosyne"—is "In a City Garden." "How strange that here is nothing as it was!" the poem's voice begins. "No, here the Past has left no residue," he muses before observing, "Yet was this willow here." He is not alone in seeking something, "Some vestige of the living that was theirs . . . / Some hint or remnant, echo, clue—some thing, / Some very little thing of what was they." No surprise, I think, to the reader of "Eride," that "Here in this place . . . / She, as a cloud / All sunrise-coloured and alone, / Thro' the blue summer trembling came to me." But he knows this is only a memory and at the same time isn't only that. "I came today to find her, I came back . . . / To her, / I came, I knew she was not here: / Now let me go. / I came because I love her so."

Is it not strange
That here in part and whole

The faithful eye sees all things as before.
For past the newer flowers,
Above the recent trees and clouds come o'er
Love finds the other hours
Once more.

This seems clearly the "she" of "Eride" and "Once"—which supposes, of course, that the relevant poems are recollections and offerings rather than pure fictions. Of course, in the absence of certainty as to the specifics of Stickney's love life, some will say "fiction," safe in the truth that poetry does not have to be autobiographical. But after many readings (the reader is invited to the same), I am convinced the recollection is real. As C.S. Lewis once suggested when arguing that the *Gospel of Saint John* is more than a theological narrative, and is instead a distinct memory: *If you don't see that, you simply don't know how to read.*

The now-old New Criticism of the last century tells us we should ignore such biographical questions and matters of authorial intention, but since we are human beings blessed with curiosity instead of citizens of the English Department . . . *who was she?*

There seem to be two real possibilities and one faint candidate. The faint one was an older married woman, "Ethel," a friend of the Stickney family, with whom Trumbull fell in love when a student at Harvard. A more enticing possibility (for reasons which become apparent) referred to by Shane Leslie was "Gifford Pinchot's sister," like Stickney himself, "very tall and good looking." Pinchot was an American conservationist, later governor of Pennsylvania. His sister was Lady Antoinette Pinchot Johnstone, wife of an Englishman somewhat older than she, and, as the slightly grainy photo online ("the Pinchot family") reveals, a doe-eyed pensive beauty, no question about it, all six feet of her to go with Stickney's six-and-a-third. But the affair was in Stickney's last year or so in Paris before his return to Cambridge, and since "Eride" was composed in the late 1890s, Antoinette Johnstone could only possibly have touched "Once," 1902, or better yet, "In a City Garden," 1904. Since that was the year Stickney was slowly dying, I find it easy enough to believe that memories of Antoinette could easily have been super-imposed upon the memories of the heroine of "Eride"—or the other way around.

And who was she? Honors go to Haldane's heroic labor and speculation (while not certainty): "The impression which emerges from the poems is of a woman of the world, Stickney's equal in intelligence and emotional depth, unusually independent and active. And it seems she had the means and strength to follow her own inclinations and lead her own life." Trumbull's younger brother, Henry, says Haldane, recalled an episode from 1896, when "Eride" was being composed. Stickney was dining with his family in Paris when "a mysterious girl arrived at the door demanding to see him." His parents foolishly forbade him to answer, which Stickney simply ignored, because they considered her "disreputable." The "affair caused lasting disapproval in the Stickney family." Since the parents controlled the purse strings, and Stickney had not a dime which they did not dole out (an attempt to gain a diplomatic post while a student at the Sorbonne went nowhere), Haldane surmises that marriage was beyond Stickney's realistic possibilities before he had much later and too late a Harvard salary.

But Trumbull told Henry years later that he should have married her. Not incidentally, the "disreputable" woman was Jewish. Which raises an intriguing possibility. Since as I indicated much earlier the name *Eridé* evidently serves as a first name only or primarily in Lithuania, might not "Eride" be not only the title of the sequence, but the appellation of the difficult heroine as well, that is to say, a *Litvak*, a Lithuanian Jewess? That specific being a possibility or not, it pleases me for reasons beyond summary to believe that this was "she." And what argument, pray tell, is there against it? If I could change history, I would volunteer to be the Dreyfusard Stickney's match-maker.

In a literary world woefully deficient in *poetic* drama, no matter how strong the naturalistic theatre of the twentieth century and beyond, it is a great loss that Stickney's were never completed. What was to be "The Cardinal Play" (working title I suppose) is evidenced in one scene and five brief fragments. Another on the life of Emperor Julian "survives" in twenty-two pages of blank verse, which end abruptly with Julian saying, "You know not what it is to be alone; / You know it not," with that last half line completed by another character, "Oh, God forgive you this." Oh God, I'd like to know how it ended.

Now, I am well aware that I have made no convincing connection with saying what cannot be said (a connection I have implied much earlier), excluding some possibly dubious fancy work with the mysterious title of "Eride." So, but . . .

I have lamented the fact that so many of Stickney's poems are fragments, but the truth is that the fragments—especially the briefest of them, from 21 lines to four—are some of the most stunning, remarkable, and provocative of Stickney's work, perhaps the four-line fragment most of all. But before I go there, I would like to return to my characterization of Stickney as one the most heart-breaking of poets.

Whatever he was feeling when his scholarly European sojourn was over—Santayana, still professor of philosophy at Harvard when Stickney returned to Cambridge, thought him somehow wounded and at odds with himself—he was still hard at work aesthetically and as a teacher, implementing many plans for publication and for instructional duties. But by his second semester . . . there was too much to do, so much unfinished, and it was quickly apparent that time was running out. In early spring, he was crippled by fatigue and headaches; his vision was increasingly impaired as well as his hearing. (All the worse for a lyrical poet!). His letters suggest a growing despair, and despair is often a way of knowing. He soon knew the worst thing, as the brain tumor was diagnosed in early summer. His friends Lodge and Moody attended him—as he continued to write through all. Doctors feared emotional calamities and tried to restrict visits. Nonetheless, Stickney received his old mentor and friend

Sylvain Lévi, although now totally blind. Stickney touched Lévi's face and . . . "*O mon papa Sylvain.*" I find it impossible to imagine a fraction, a fragment, of all that was going through Trumbull's mind—and I would rather not suffer the pain of even attempting. But I am sure that one thing that pained him was the certainty that he had not said all the ineffable things he wished to say.

We do know what Stickney was writing in the nine months he was alive in 1904, with only half those nine, at most, in anything approaching bearable health. One thing of course, as I have mentioned, was "In a City Garden," where he was clearly revisiting one and perhaps two of his great beloveds, in a pain beyond my imagining. Will Moody, in an essay on his old friend in *The North American Review* in 1906, wrote of "In a City Garden:" "There is in Stickney's lyric utterance at its best something momentously unspoken, which betrays to deeper abysses of feeling than are advertised of, which causes the reader, if he be sensitive to such suggestion, to turn and wonder what it is so soul-shaking under the innocent words." But Moody could easily have been speaking of five other pieces which Stickney left unfinished in his last year: five fragments, apparently lines from a play in his head since one of them begins "Enter X, who learns the dispute and says . . ."

The fragments are essentially metaphysical speculations, as for instance one says in part:

> I used to think
> The mind essential in the body, even
> As stood the body essential in the mind:
> Two inseparable things, by nature equal
> And similar, and in creation's song
> Halving the total scale; it is not so.

How typical of Stickney to be dramatically imagining one of the metaphysical problems most notoriously difficult to talk about, called in philosophy "the mind-body problem." Another fragment, entitled "Blindness and Deafness," I prefer to pass over in silence.

A third, called "The Soul of Time," the longest, begins:

> Time's a circumference
> Whereof the segment of our station seems
> A long straight line from nothing into naught.
> Therefore we say "progress," "infinity"—

before the odd shift from such heavy rhetorical weight to the near dismissive and charming:

> Dull words whose object
> Hangs in the air of error and delights
> Our boyish minds ahunt for butterflies.

The speaker becomes more assertive, with difficult metaphysical metaphors (or "conceits," as literary criticism used to have it), "a better distribution / Between the dreaming mind and real truth"—to which someone intervenes with "I cannot understand you." The speaker answers:

> 'Tis because
> You lean over my meaning's edge and feel
> A dizziness of the things I have not said.

The fourth fragment is of a different mood altogether, a moment of. . . what? Peace? Loveliness, whatever it is:

> Be patient, very patient, for the skies
> Within my human soul now sunset-flushed
> Break desperate magic on the world I know,
> And in the crimson evening flying down
> Bell-sounds and birds of ancient ecstasy
> Most wonderfully carol one time more.

But, then, the fifth fragment: by legend—and why not?—the last thing Trumbull Stickney wrote. By convention it is thought to be poetic expression of Stickney's recognition of his mortality, a brave facing of death. Well, I think not, not exactly; I think it an attempt rather to put the essence of a general human vulnerability into words. How does one talk about vulnerability? Seems a very easy question. So . . . how? The problem is that when one tries to say this unsayable thing, one can tend to utter banalities trying to assert a brave looking-whatever-in-the-face, or if one is not careful, one can tend to sound simply paranoid. Stickney prefers to express this ineffable thing another way.

> Sir, say no more.
> Within me 'tis as if
> The green and climbing eyesight of a cat
> Crawled near my mind's poor birds.

SCHOPENHAUER: REFLECTIONS ON A
FLAWED PHILOSOPHER

KENNETH FRANCIS

THE GERMAN PESSIMISTIC philosopher Arthur Schopenhauer (1788-1860) tapped into the terrors of existence
with graphic clarity and superb emotional prose like no other
philosopher before him or after his death, with the arguable exception of Romanian-born philosopher, Emil Cioran.

Cioran said: "If I were to be totally sincere, I would say that I
do not know why I live and why I do not stop living. The answer
probably lies in the irrational character of life which maintains

47

itself without reason."[1]

Less defeatist than Cioran; however, besides art, one of Schopenhauer's reasons for living was to express such worldly horrors in his greatest work, *The World as Will and Representation*,[2] which is like the *Book of Ecclesiastes* on steroids. He wrote about such horrors in all five continents, where every second of every minute of every hour of every day, millions of carnivorous beasts are tearing each other to pieces alive in a world of perpetual screaming. This is how he viewed the hellish bloodbath of grotesque survival in the wild. "The agony of the devoured animal is always far greater than the pleasure of the devourer," he wrote.

And as compassionate humans, one can surely sympathise with Schopenhauer's bleak words, despite his anthropomorphising such animal suffering. There is nothing more grotesque in the wild than seeing a pack of hungry hyenas feasting on a dying wildebeest, with its lower entrails hanging outside its body, while the hyenas tear them apart to the groans of the beast watching itself being eaten alive.

But it's not just Schopenhauer's sharp perception and bleak view of life that make his work so impressive. His incredible prose also inspired waves of the world's greatest writers and thinkers of the nineteenth and twentieth centuries.

As a young adult atheist, when I first read Schopenhauer some 35 years ago, I was greatly impressed by his excellent description of suffering in the world. I remember at the time thinking how cruel it was to bring children into such a horrible existence, and, in my philosophically unsophisticated worldview, I thought that procreation was morally wrong. As Schopenhauer wrote:

> If children were brought into the world by an act of pure reason alone, would the human race continue to exist? Would not a man rather have so much sympathy with the coming

---

1 Emil Cioran, *On the Heights of Despair*, 1934.

2 Arthur Schopenhauer, *The World as Will and Representation* (WWR; German: *Die Welt als Wille und Vorstellung*, WWV), 1818.

generation as to spare it the burden of existence, or at any
rate not take it upon himself to impose that burden upon it
in cold blood?[3]

On atheism, this seems to make sense, but it's flawed because on naturalism, we wouldn't have freedom of the will to
choose whether or not to procreate. We would be no different
than animals, who copulate without reflection on whether or
not to do so.

Schopenhauer says human life must be some kind of mistake. The truth of this will be sufficiently obvious if we only remember that man is a compound of needs and necessities hard
to satisfy:

> [A]nd that even when they are satisfied, all he obtains is a
> state of painlessness, where nothing remains to him but aban-
> donment to boredom. This is direct proof that existence has
> no real value in itself; for what is boredom but the feeling of
> the emptiness of life? If life—the craving for which is the very
> essence of our being—were possessed of any positive intrin-
> sic value, there would be no such thing as boredom at all:
> mere existence would satisfy us in itself, and we should want
> for nothing.[4]

But when I reverted back to Christianity, procreation took
on a new meaning: Human life is not some kind of mistake,
because God doesn't make mistakes; some individuals do. As
for humans being a compound of needs and necessities hard to
satisfy, along with boredom and the emptiness of life: On Christianity, it's not this life that ultimately matters, but the afterlife of
bliss through the Beatific Vision. This world is a cosmic "waiting
room" ever since the Fall of Eden. Even Schopenhauer seems to
allude to the above when he writes of the possibility of life being
better if it had intrinsic value, but where he fails is that there can
only be intrinsic value to human life through objective moral

---

3 Arthur Schopenhauer, *Studies in Pessimism: The Essays*, published by
George Allen & Company, LTD, London, 1913.

4 Ibid.

values and duties. And that can only be obtained through God.

As for his philosophy: it is a strange mixture of pantheism (the universe is "god" but not personal), panpsychism/panentheism (everything is conscious; for Schopenhauer, possibly a kind of God-type Will), solipsism (only one's mind exists), and Idealism (the so-called "physical external world" is dependent on consciousness). Also, there are those who see elements of Buddhism and Hinduism in his philosophy.

However, despite this metaphorical melting pot of metaphysical concepts, the core of Schopenhauer's driving cosmic force is an aggressive Will, blindly kicking its way through the universe, devouring everything in its path—a cosmic psycho, who just keeps rolling along.

Schopenhauer laments this sorry state of affairs, especially, as mentioned, the suffering in the animal kingdom, and, despite his misanthropic contempt of humans, he says we can sometimes momentarily escape it by contemplating/perceiving works of great art.

But let us return to Schopenhauer's concern for animals devouring one another: When a hungry lion kills its prey, the king of the jungle kills the beast, but doesn't murder it. In Schopenhauer's godless universe, there are no objective moral agents, and every scream of agony is nothing more than a brute fact of nature.

Philosophy professor Tim Madigan said:

> Schopenhauer occupies an anomalous position in the history of philosophy. His writings are a peculiar mixture of rigorous analysis of concepts, idiosyncratic interpretations of previous systems, and biting attacks on his enemies. For much of his life he was ignored, and most of the copies of his 1844 masterwork *The World as Will and Representation*, in Nietzsche's words 'had to be turned into wastepaper ...'

> No wonder his trust and love for his fellow humans was so low. And yet, surprisingly enough, Schopenhauer – along with his philosophical hero David Hume – was one of the first Western philosophers to emphasize compassion as the

basis of morality.[5]

But here's the problem: Where does this morality come from? The theistic worldview is quite clear on this: 1. Without God, objective moral values and duties do not exist. 2. But objective moral values and duties do exist. 3. Therefore, God exists.

Schopenhauer's ideas of morality lie in human compassion, not God, whom he doesn't believe in. The problem here is compassion can be subjective, a matter of taste. Schopenhauer would disagree, saying: "If an action has as its motive an egoistic aim, it cannot have any moral worth."

But surely egoism and compassion can be linked? One good person's sense of pity for a creature's suffering at the jaws of a lion is another person's feeling of compassion for the lion's daily struggle for survival. But it's not only animal welfare that Schopenhauer was concerned about. He was a man of great moral indignation, but without objective moral justification. The question is: Was his moral indignation subjective, thus, solipsistic? If so, the absurd conclusion to this leads to a spiritual war inside one's head with the negative figments of one's imagination: Fighting with…er, oneself!

Schopenhauer wrote: "The world is my representation… [man] does not know a sun and an earth, but only an eye that sees a sun, a hand that feels an earth; that the world around him is there only as representation, in other words, only in reference to another thing, namely that which represents, and this is himself."[6] Does this sound like a form of solipsism?

Schopenhauer again: "Since everything which exists or happens for a man exists only in his consciousness and happens for it alone, the most essential thing for a man is the constitution of this consciousness."[7]

Although this unproven concept is quite interesting and po-

---

5 Tim Madigan, "Essay from Thoughts Out Of Season, 'Schopenhauer as Educator', 1874; Schopenhauer's Compassionate Morality," *Philosophy Now*, 2005.

6 *The World as Will and Representation*.

7 Arthur Schopenhauer, *The Wisdom of Life and Counsels and Maxims*, 1851.

tentially profound, we don't have the existential luxury to live our lives by theorising on such matters. In other words, we have to improve our lives, especially spiritually. Why? Because our immortal soul is at risk of eternal damnation. And unfortunately, metaphorical spiritual "eternal damnation assurance" is one of the steps to Heaven.

According to the Irish philosopher George Berkeley, who wasn't a solipsist but didn't believe in the physical "external world," God or religion is the basis for improving one's life, not damaging it, and a common-sense view of life is the best path to achieving such a goal. Berkeley was unique and quite happy in his philosophical world view, while he thought other philosophers throughout history were usually frustrated and complicated matters by analysing everything beyond the reach of human reasoning.

Being reasonable for Berkeley is acknowledging that the only "real" things that exist in the world are spirits who are created by an infinite Spirit, God. Put simply, the whole of reality is mental (certainly in the year 2020, in more ways than one).

Schopenhauer was an atheist, but Berkeley hated atheism and wanted to put God center stage, acknowledging that an Absolute Observer must reign supreme over perceiving reality. Such a supernatural eternal Absolute Entity would not require the multiplication of causes beyond what is necessary to explain itself.

Berkeley was a Christian, and his Idealism[8] encompasses other "sub" minds, a kind of community of souls in a non-physical realm. In the end, hologram or no hologram, speculation or scepticism on the universe and the world are a waste of time. Life is short, and to lose your eternal soul sitting on the fence of agnosticism is worse than tragic if God exists.

Hebrews 11:3 tells us, "By faith we understand that the universe was created by the word of God, so that what is seen was

---

8   George Berkeley wrote *A Treatise Concerning the Principles of Human Knowledge* in 1710, which, after its poor reception, he rewrote in dialogue form and published under the title *Three Dialogues between Hylas and Philonous* in 1713.

not made out of things that are visible." A faith in God based
on reason and trust (not blind faith) is all we need for physical,
spiritual fulfilment and truth. The truth is more important than
a world view you want to live with based on a false perception
that is "my reality."

Despite being a misogynistic curmudgeon, and the flaws in
his philosophy, Schopenhauer found something to smile about
in the world's best-loved creatures: the humble dog. He owned
a succession of poodles and anyone who is familiar with such
breeds will be aware of their great intelligence.

A misanthropic loner, I've no doubt that when the great
grumpy man was out for a walk with his favourite pooch, "Atma,"
Schopenhauer's grumpy guard would drop, as walkers, like they
usually do when seeing a dog, would stop and have a jovial chat
about the creature, asking about his habits or any funny story
to liven up their spirits. At least they wouldn't dampen their
moods by moaning over the horrors of perpetual screaming in
the great four continents of the world. I'd like to think his dogs
gave him some solace from his bleak world view without hope.

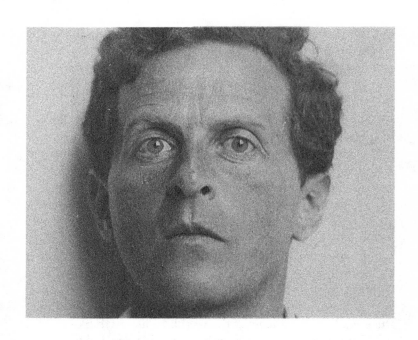

LUDWIG WITTGENSTEIN (1889-1951)

THEODORE DALRYMPLE

NO ONE WOULD DISSENT from the proposition that Ludwig Wittgenstein was a highly peculiar person. By all accounts he was about as comfortable to be with as is a pebble in a shoe. However splendid or otherwise comfortable the shoe might be, a pebble in it is impossible to ignore and the sensation it causes drives everything else from the mind.

Whether or how far a philosopher's character affects or even determines his philosophy is a matter of speculation. Was Hume equable because his philosophy was cool and ironic, or was his philosophy cool and ironic because he was equable? Could one imagine Marx propagating a pacifist philosophy, or was he a stormy petrel in search of a doctrine to justify his violent passions and desire for domination?[1]

Wittgenstein was both impressive and admirable, but not altogether likeable. His probity was evident, but he was a tortured soul, and tortured souls are not always good company, unlike a murderer of my acquaintance who chopped up his best friend and when asked how he would describe his own character said that he was "laid back and fun to be with."

Wittgenstein had a powerful sense of morality, but he was not always good or even good-natured in the conventional sense. Born into an enormously rich family—his father was the greatest steel magnate of the then Austro-Hungarian Empire—he gave all his fortune away, though not to the poor despite being a socialist, but rather to members of his own family. Nor was he particularly empathetic to the travails of all the poor. He detested the peasants of that part of Austria in which he went to teach schoolchildren, after he thought that he had solved all the problems of philosophy once and for all (a rather peculiar, almost megalomanic thought of the kind that Karl Marx suffered, or made others, suffer from). He extended little comprehension to the peasants, whom he regarded as backward, bigoted and materialistic in the worst and crudest sense. He antagonised them by his mode of life and seemed not to realise that if he wanted their co-operation in the new and reformist teaching methods that he adopted, he ought to have been in some way conciliatory and understanding towards them, rather than making his disdain for them at least implicitly clear. He was almost autistic in his lack of social graces, but of course such diagnoses are mainly redescriptions, or shorthand for certain characteristics, rather than having much explanatory value.

---

1 "Gradually it has become clear to me what every great philosophy so far has been: namely, the personal confession of its author and a kind of involuntary and unconscious memoir; also that the moral (or immoral) intentions in every philosophy constituted the real germ of life from which the whole plant has grown." – Nietzsche, *Beyond Good and Evil*. That Nietzsche said it is for me prima facie evidence that it is false, or at least exaggerated; but one must remember that if Hitler himself said that two and two were four, two and two would still be four.

Wittgenstein's teaching methods were original for their time and were apparently successful in their results. When teaching grammar, he employed examples from the local dialect rather than from High German. He thought that what he taught should be relevant to the children's present or future likely experience. In this, he was a forerunner of some modern pedagogy which, when hollowed out in the hands or mouths of less brilliant teachers than Wittgenstein, has the effect of enclosing children in the very limited world that they already know. Wittgenstein's success as a teacher of children was probably not generalizable because he was so extraordinary a man, much as the success of psychotherapy, where it is successful, is more the consequence of the therapist's personality and ability to create a rapport with the patient than of the psychological theory according to which he or she practices. Wittgenstein craved affection but found it difficult to express it; he evidently came nearest with children.[2]

Wittgenstein became the centre of a cult, as did another Viennese whom he was too uncritically to admire, Sigmund Freud.[3] Highly intelligent people imitated Wittgenstein's style and his manner, though it seems to me that he adopted a dog-

---

2 In 1926, he was tried for assault on a child. Wittgenstein was not so much in advance of his times that he did not resort to corporal chastisement of children. But there is no indication other than the accusation itself, of which he was acquitted, that he was more prone to its use than any other teacher of the time. It is probable that the accusation was made in a spirit of malice towards him.

3 That Freud was very far from truthful is now established beyond reasonable doubt. Borch-Jacobsen has investigated his so-called therapeutic results with forensic exactitude and shown all of Freud's claims not only to have been bogus, but such as he must have known to be false. This does not quite make Freud necessarily a charlatan because many people may become so enamoured of their own theories, and so genuinely convinced of their truth, that mere empirical facts that go against them seem like temporary obstacles in the path of higher truth. Most of us are procrustean to some extent. There are obvious connections—I almost said family resemblances—between the work of Freud and Wittgenstein. Freud sought to dissolve away repressions and resistances that allegedly led to neurosis, and Wittgenstein sought to dissolve away the misuse of language that allegedly resulted in bogus puzzles that actually referred to nothing but nevertheless consumed a lot of time and mental energy.

in-the-manger to life, at least in certain respects. He cared not for dress, or rather he cared to demonstrate that he cared not for dress, which is not quite the same thing. A person who carefully rejects the conventions of his time, place, class and nation cannot be said not to care about them; and whether his conduct, or in this case, dress, represents an improvement must be assessed according to moral or aesthetic judgment. It seems pretty clear that Wittgenstein adopted his mode of dress as a matter of principle, for example, never wearing a necktie and hardly changing his attire according to the social circumstances in which it was worn, so the question must be asked whether, if others adopted his principles, would the world be a better place? The answer, I think, is that it would be a pretty dismal one, though he was undoubtedly, as a matter of sociological fact, ahead of his time in his militant informality. If, on the other hand, his mode of dress was merely that of personal taste, a kind of aesthetic private language as it were, and not the consequence of a moral outlook or principle, it was purely egoistic. I am reminded of Doctor Johnson's stricture in his short biography of Jonathan Swift:

> Singularity, as it implies a contempt of the general practice is a kind of defiance which justly provokes the hostility of ridicule; he, therefore, who indulges in peculiar traits, is worse than others, if he be not better.

One may admire Wittgenstein's powers of self-denial, his capacity to live (as he sometimes did) on his own in the wilds of Norway, able even, or especially, in isolation to consider fundamental problems of philosophy, and his uninterest in worldly rewards, but a world according to Wittgensteinian example would be a cold and humourless place, without affection. One can see this from the house in Vienna that he had a hand in designing for his sister. So utterly without ornamentation was it that it makes Le Corbusier's concrete towers seem almost Rococo by comparison; it also looks as if it were constructed as a bacteriological or virological laboratory rather than as a home for ordinary human beings. It is to be noted that Wittgenstein, in helping to design and build it, was not so much interested in the construction of an individual home, as in creating a design or template for all building; but to live in a city of Wittgensteinian buildings would be like living in a vast refrigerator. In fact, his eschewal of ornamentation—in this, of course, he was neither original nor alone—was implicitly barbarian and inhuman, unless there were some reasoned argument as to why, at the precise time he was designing and building, ornamentation of any and all kinds should be avoided. There can be no such argument, at least no valid argument; in other words, his house in Vienna is a manifestation of an inhuman taste, if not of mental pathology. Certainly, if the world had been Wittgensteinian in its building aesthetic from the dawn of civilisation, there would not have existed much man-made beauty in the world.

No man is obliged to be clubbable, but no man should think of himself as in any way better than his fellows for not being clubbable, and Wittgenstein's austerity was certainly not without its dose of pride and sense of superiority. His manner of dominating philosophical discussions in Cambridge could be interpreted as an exceptional urge to truth, but alternatively as an urge to power; for it is certainly true that all who live modestly or self-effacingly are not modest or self-effacing.[4]

Wittgenstein was clearly a man of brilliant, original and indeed awesome powers. He spoke three languages perfectly, knew Latin and Greek, played the clarinet well, and is said to have come near to designing a jet engine while working at Manchester University. He was a gifted repairer and adapter of engines. And even if the house he helped to design and build did not coincide with my taste, he was able to design and build a house—which most people, including me, are not.

He impressed Bertrand Russell on first meeting, Russell very soon recognising that he was a man out of the ordinary. Desiccated as Russell may sometimes have appeared, he was susceptible to passionate persons. At about the same time that

---

4   It may be that his drive to dominate in part explains his ability to form better relations with the children he taught than with their parents. It is not so much that children are easier to dominate as that less effort is necessary to do so.

he and Wittgenstein formed their association, Russell also fell under the influence of D.H. Lawrence, only later to realise that Lawrence's blood and semen philosophy had unpleasant undertones and consequences.

In fact, Russell and Wittgenstein were never soulmates, or perhaps I should say were never on the same wavelength. For it seems to me that Wittgenstein was at heart always a mystic with a veneer—misperceived at that—of positivism. Ultimately, he was religious. He never accorded science the importance that Russell did, though there is no doubt that he was perfectly capable of having become a scientist.

It is generally agreed that Wittgenstein had two philosophies, linked in some indefinable way that it has been the delight of philosophical commentators to find—just as it has been the delight of Marxist philosophers to find the connections between Marx's earlier, humanistic work and his later, supposedly scientific work.

Here I must interpose a confession: I am not a philosopher, except in the sense that everyone, whether he knows it or not, has a philosophy (albeit an incoherent one), and much less am I an expert on Wittgenstein. I console myself with the fact that Wittgenstein himself had great contempt for the vast majority of professional philosophers, and invariably advised his students against a career in academic philosophy.[5] Moreover, even those who have devoted their lives to Wittgensteinian studies are not in agreement as to what he actually meant. This is reassuring to a rank amateur, of course, but it is not a license to propound absolutely *any* interpretation, for example that Wittgenstein was defending Catholic orthodoxy (or specifically attacking it, for that matter). Nevertheless, I write with trepidation and recall the African saying: when elephants fight, the ant—or maybe the grass, or both—is squashed.

---

5 As often is the case with Wittgenstein, there is an inconsistency. His seminars or lectures while he was professor of philosophy at Cambridge were attended almost overwhelmingly by a coterie of professional philosophers. It is highly unlikely that anyone else would have had the faintest idea what he was driving at; only with much exegesis did his renown spread after his death.

The famous last line of the only book he published during his lifetime, the *Tractatus Logico-Philosophicus*, at least in the first English translation, is of great beauty, and perhaps is one which everyone should always bear in mind, though it would risk cutting human conversation down by at least a half: "Whereof one cannot speak, thereof one must be silent."

This comes at the end of Wittgenstein's attempt to find the limits of language as far as factual propositions are concerned. He seemed to me to have adopted a theory that is obviously false, at least if I have even the faintest inkling of what he was trying to do.[6] He said that there must, for logical reasons, be simple propositions that are further unanalysable, all of which are non-contradictory and which go on to build more usual, everyday factual assertions, much as physical objects are made up of atoms.[7] Moreover, these simple propositions are pictorial in nature: they represent a state of affairs. Wittgenstein did not provide any example of such a simple, unanalysable proposition, which seems to me a little like signing a promissory note with no means foreseeable of paying it; but of course something that is logically necessary does not need empirical examples to prove it. I don't need to find Socrates' tomb to know that, if all men are mortal and Socrates was a man, Socrates was mortal. To go looking for empirical proof of the validity of the syllogism would be absurd.

It seems to me, though, that if all propositions are in some sense pictures of reality, true or false, and all pictures are ultimately analysable to a picture that is not further analysable, Wittgenstein is committing himself to something deeply metaphysical: namely, that there are ultimate particles, so to speak, of reality. This may or may not be the case in fact, but it has not been proved empirically to be the case, and perhaps could never be proved empirically to be the case: and so the belief that it is,

6 Brilliance is by no means incompatible with belief in bad, foolish or preposterous ideas; perhaps, even, they require a certain brilliance to be believed. The labour theory of value is one of those obviously false ideas that brilliant men such as Ricardo and Marx believed.

7 Ultimately of elementary particles, the number of which changes regularly.

or must be, the case is metaphysical, akin to the argument for the existence of God from the necessity of a first cause.[8]

Now because Wittgenstein associated with members of the Vienna Circle, he has sometimes been taken to be a logical positivist in this stage of his philosophical life. The Logical Positivists came to the conclusion that, to have meaning, a sentence had to be either true by definition, or refer to a state of affairs whose truth or falsity empirical evidence could decide, or at least upon which it had some bearing.[9] This, of course, was not a new doctrine, for Hume had written nearly two centuries before:

> If we take in our hand any volume of divinity or school meta-physics, for instance; let us ask, Does it contain any abstract reasoning concerning quantity or number? No. Does it contain any experimental reasoning concerning matter of fact and existence? No. Commit it then to the flames: for it can contain nothing but sophistry and illusion.

This passage is full of Humean irony: he was far too civilised and well-balanced a man to wish to burn books, or to believe what he said with the conviction of a martyr.[10] His ambition

---

8 It is worth quoting Swift here:
   So naturalists observe, a flea
   Hath smaller fleas that on him prey;
   And these have smaller still to bite 'em;
   And so proceed ad infinitum.
Wittgenstein, at this stage at least, would not have agreed. But he would have agreed with Sigmund Freud's drift in his paper, "Analysis Termiable and Interminable," believing that analysis, either psycho or linguistic, had to end somewhere. "Analysis must come to an end," wrote Wittgenstein in his notebooks; the need or wish was father to the thought. Psychoanalysts, for obvious economic reasons, often forget this need, their wish being opposite.

9 Any empirical evidence in favour of a proposition might, of course, be insufficient to prove a proposition, but all empirical evidence whatsoever could not be irrelevant to its truth. If I say that there is a fox in the garden, I might adduce in favour of the proposition that there is a reddish-furred animal, of doggish size and shape, in the garden. This is not conclusive evidence, but it is not irrelevant either.

10 In *Three Guineas*, Virginia Woolf advocated burning whole libraries

was to clear away the mental cobwebs, as he saw them, of metaphysics and metaphysical systems. It is notable that Marx also used the word *metaphysical* as a term of intellectual abuse, and Wittgenstein, although he changed his mind on many things, never lost the ambition to clear away, by a kind of psychoanalytical method deploying logic, all philosophical—which is to say metaphysical—problems which he saw as mere confusions caused by misuse of, or the misapprehension of the role of, language.

Although he was often taken to be, at this stage is his life, in some sense a logical positivist, he clearly was not: he was more mystic than scientistic. Although he claimed that all that could be said could be said clearly, he thought that the most important things in life could not be said. Only the lesser truths, mundane in the most literal sense, can be articulated in language; the rest, as Hamlet put it, is silence.

This seems to me not only false, but obviously false, and very thin into the bargain. Of course, the undesirable consequences of a proposition do not make it false; thus if all that Wittgenstein said (at this stage) were true, it would be no argument against it that it would have terrible consequences. It is no proof of the existence of God that if it were true that if God did not exist everything would be permitted, and we desire very strongly that everything should not be permitted. Truth is not compliance with what we should like to be the case.

There is no doubt that Wittgenstein wrestled with the angel of hidden truth, so to speak, with an intensity that not many men are capable of,[11] in order to produce his *Tractatus*; but effort, even by a person of the greatest brilliance such as he, is not accomplishment. Of course, failure in philosophy is not to be reprehended, that is to say, failure to elaborate a philosophy that answers once and for all, indubitably, the questions of philosophy that have bemused mankind for two and a half millennia at least; however, it does seem to me that to declare that one has

---

down, not only once, but regularly, every time they were reconstituted. Given her condition of resentment, I am not convinced that she was being ironical.

11 Certainly not I.

solved all the problems of philosophy (actually, *dissolved* them) once and for all, and to conduct a part of one's subsequent life as if this were indeed so, points to a defect of character. Every man believes his beliefs to be true, of course, otherwise they would not be his beliefs, but few are so convinced of the wholeness of their truth that they think that there is nothing further to be said on the matters to which they pertain. For me, at any rate, there is a frightening intensity to the stare in his eyes captured in photographs, as if he were a kind of Savonarola come to preach against the wickedness, or at least the conceptual laxity, of *all* previous philosophers.

There is a certain kind of person—I have met one or two—whose radical changes of opinion never affect the certainty with which they hold them, their certainty being like the grin of the Cheshire cat, that which remains when everything else has disappeared. Yes, they might have been mistaken formerly; but no, they cannot possibly be mistaken now. Whatever inner doubts Wittgenstein may have had about his ideas, he always treated those who disagreed as if they were *ex officio* wrong.

Anyway, Wittgenstein gave up his picture theory of language, which was an attempt to find the grounds of logical certainty for at least propositional language. With it, he ended by implying that it was all right to say that the cat sat on the mat but not that it is wrong to commit genocide. The latter is an illegitimate attempt to say in words something that belongs to the realm of silence. His realm of what could not be said was like a black hole for most of human discourse: nothing that went into it could ever come out.

As I have said, it is pretty obvious that the picture theory of language must be wrong. If we take a statement such as "My love is like a red, red rose," it is neither strictly empirical nor utterly meaningless in that it conveys no sense at all to the listener or reader. We should regard someone who set out to find a red, red rose that resembled my love in some way, or tried to enumerate the ways, as being mad. Would my love be like a red, red rose once our investigator found that she shares 50 per cent of her DNA with a rose? And what is the difference between a red, red rose and a merely red one? What should we think of someone who went to a rose garden in order to find out? And yet, at the same time, "my love is like a red rose" does not have the same meaning, or connotation, as "my love is like a red, red rose." Albeit that the intensifying repetition of the word "red" is not merely empirical, it would not be true either that it was completely without an empirical aspect, for there are red roses of which one would not say "that is a red, red rose," and others of which one might say it. But I doubt that anyone would take measurements of the light wavelengths that would make a rose not merely "red," but "red, red," even in these times of heightened academic futility.

"My love" also places limits on the possible meaning of the sentence. It is unlikely that "My love" would be an ugly shrew, though this is not altogether excluded, since ugly shrews have, in fact, sometimes been loved; but these are a young man's words (we know this from our experience of life), and we imagine her to be beautiful rather than ugly, however much we may believe that, in theory, beauty is in the eye of the beholder.

The sentence is clearly not without meaning, in the sense that it conveys something to the reader or listener; and certainly it has a pictorial element. I doubt if anyone could read or hear the words without conjuring up an image of a beautiful young woman, and certainly a deep red rose; but I doubt also that anyone would fail to understand the deep emotion in these words, even if he or she had never experienced the emotion in question. It would not be exactly the same emotion as that of the writer—we would not ourselves be in love with the subject of them—but in some sense, and to a degree, we know what he is feeling, or think that we do.

There is obviously a lot of fuzziness about this statement, and it requires quite a lot of context in order for it to make any sense, if not an indubitable or final sense. We need to know, for example, that young men are inclined to fall in love with young women, that love is an emotion that can swallow up all other considerations, and that young men go about saying such things, at least if they are of a certain level of mental cultivation.

But they are also of a certain culture; it is for anthropologists to discover whether there are cultures in which such sentiments are never felt or uttered.[12]

Wittgenstein, having tried to create a system in which the world was mirrored exactly, so to speak, by a system of linguistic expression, leaving no space for meaningful language to do anything else, such matters as ethics and aesthetics being relegated, or elevated, to a numinous world beyond the ability of language to say anything about it, eventually came to an almost diametrically opposite view, namely that there was no means by which we could construct such a language, and in fact it was the world that mirrored our language rather than the other way round. Marx believed that it was our interests that determined our thoughts about the world; Wittgenstein (if I have understood correctly, which I freely admit that I may not have done[13])

---

12   If they were never uttered, I suppose the later Wittgenstein would say, they would never be felt. Compare this with La Rochefoucauld's remark that most people would never fall in love if they had never heard of it.

13   In which case, I would hardly be the first or the last one. Wittgenstein exegesis remains a minor industry. I have among my books about Wittgenstein, not a specialist library I hasten to add, books about Wittgenstein the religious thinker and Wittgenstein the Marxist, or at least about Wittgenstein the Marxist-compatible and -reinforcing. Wittgenstein did indeed contemplate emigrating to Russia, though probably more in search of virtuous egalitarian discomfort to assuage his unassuageable guilt than out of adherence to any deep ideology. When he visited Russia, he recognised that, notwithstanding his developing views about language and its relation to reality, the oppression was real enough and not merely part of a language game. That oppression could even be written about—and was. He returned to the safer purlieus of Cambridge, where a number of academics were soon to do their best to bring such oppression to Britain. The point is that if Wittgenstein could be viewed as both a religious and Marxist thinker (I exclude the sociological observation that Marxism as an ideology and movement came itself to bear considerable resemblances to a religion), what he was trying to say could not have been altogether clear. This, perhaps, was another reason for his famous dispute in Cambridge with Karl Popper during which a poker was, or was not, waved at Popper by Wittgenstein. The former always thought that it was more than an intellectual virtue, but a moral duty, to make what one was saying as clear as possible, to render it open to argument. Whatever Popper's defects of character (and who is without them?), I side decisively with Popper on this issue. Not that Popper was incapable of unnecessary ambiguity: he once wrote, re-

came to the view that, in essence, there were only different types of language, or language games, that were incommensurable so that it was impossible to say whether one reflected the world more truly or faithfully than another. Language was all that there was.

It is surely no new discovery, or perhaps I should say, doctrine, that words cannot be pinned down to indubitable, iron-clad meanings. Aristotle, at the beginning of his *Ethics*, says that words should not be made to bear more precision than they are capable of bearing. It is obvious that when we read "My love is like a red, red rose" that it is not meant literally, but also that it is not meant to convey nothing about the world. Again, take some lines from Shakespeare's *Sonnet Cxxxvii*:

> When my love swears that she is made of truth
> I do believe her though I know she lies...

Surely this cannot mean anything, for it contains a contradiction. To say x is untrue, but I believe x, is absurd. And yet, these lines not only mean something, but mean a great deal. The poem continues:

> That she may think me some untutour'd youth
> Unlearnèd in the world's false subtleties.

First, this suggests the existence of a phenomenon psychologists call *cognitive dissonance*; second, it suggests that it is a fluctuating rather than a permanent state, for it is when my love swears that she is made of truth, not all the time, that I believe her though I know she lies; and third, that this peculiar state of mind is brought about by a wish, namely to make her believe that I am not experienced in what the Nigerians call "the game of love," though obviously I am so experienced otherwise

---

garding the meeting in Cambridge, "my last meeting with Wittgenstein." This was not strictly a lie: it was his last meeting with Wittgenstein, but it was also his first and only meeting with Wittgenstein, while the locution implies but does not assert otherwise. I think Wittgenstein might have delighted in this ambiguity, though he was long dead by the time Popper employed it.

I would not need to cover it up, and that I am an innocent and therefore do not recognise her lies. The belief in untruths is reciprocal:

> Thus vainly thinking that she thinks me young
> Although she knows my days are past their best,
> Simply I credit her false-speaking tongue:
> On both sides thus is simple truth suppress'd.

This ability to believe what we know to be false is essential to human happiness, at least in the matter of lasting love:

> But wherefore says she not she is unjust?
> And wherefore say not I that I am old?
> O, loves best habit is in seeming trust,
> And age in love loves not to have years told:
>   Therefore I lie with her and she with me,
>   And in our faults by lies we flatter'd be.

This has profound implications for human intercourse and the language in which it is expressed. Here, if anywhere, is a language game such as Wittgenstein subsequently thought that we were engaged upon all the time when we use language, though according to him, there were many different games. The purpose of this Shakespearian game is to conceal what we know to be true, both from others and, to an extent, from ourselves, for the obvious reason that it allows a desirable situation to persist—which it never could if we blurted out our thoughts as and when we had them, couched in the most literal language of which a person is capable. How long would the poet's love last if he were to reply, "I know you're lying?"

But when the orthopaedic surgeon tells his patient that his femur is broken and that he will repair it, is his language any kind of a game, really indistinguishable, ontologically, from that of "My love is like a red, red rose?" Is not its relation to the world a fairly close and unambiguous one?

I am a naïve realist to the extent that I believe in the reality of oppression in the Soviet Union, or of the therapeutic effectiveness in some circumstances of antibiotics, or of the destructive power of nuclear weapons, or even of hard-boiled eggs against soft-boiled eggs according to length of time of boiling at the same elevation and atmospheric pressure. Unless the use of language had, at least potentially, some ability to express a close relationship to the world, it is difficult to see, except by an astonishing series of coincidences, how scientific progress in understanding could have taken place.

In other words, one of the language games is to convey a picture of the world, and in this it is capable of being successful, though it is also capable of the greatest obfuscation. As to Wittgenstein's persistent belief, which he arrived at early but never renounced, that philosophical questions are merely puzzles that can be dissolved away, I believe it to be utterly false. The difference between a deontological and consequentialist morality, for example, seems to me perfectly comprehensible and real and deep, and just because no decisive argument can be produced in favour of either affects neither the reality nor the depth of the difference.[14] Human beings are condemned, if that is quite the word, *not* to be silent whereof they cannot speak.

Wittgenstein's argument against the existence of private languages seems to me either false or trivial.[15] It seems to me to flirt with a kind of behaviourism, the latter being a shallow, though for a time predominant, school of psychology. In essence, it says that no one would know what pain was because no one would know the meaning of the word pain unless someone in the user's life had exclaimed, "Ouch!" And, say, withdrawn his limb from whatever it was that had caused him to say, "Ouch!" The meaning of the word is the use of the word.

This is surely mistaken. We should not say that a person who had no language for one reason or another was incapable of feeling pain. Some people feel pain without expressing it (I have done so myself) and some express it without feeling

---

14 Wittgenstein never denied the pertinence of morality. Indeed, much of his life could be interpreted as a struggle with a kind of hyper-morality, in other words, an exaggeration of the demands of morality.

15 Bertrand Russell failed to see the significance of Wittgenstein's later work.

it. Moreover, pain is not a unitary phenomenon, either pain or not pain. It has so many varieties, intensities and qualities that we rely on a person to describe what he is feeling. It is true that his behaviour may sometimes tell us something about some or other quality of what he is feeling, for example, colicky pain may cause the sufferer to expostulate at intervals. But as every doctor knows (and is taught), the quality of a person's pain is an important aid to diagnosis, and in the great majority of patients who are not hypochondriacs or malingerers, their description of their pain correlates highly with pathology from which they suffer. No amount of observation of their behaviour will tell the observer what the patient is experiencing. To provide a description, the patient must consult his own experiences, and this may not be straightforward or instantaneous for him.[16] Moreover, he can be mistaken in his use of language, he can misdescribe what he is feeling.

In other words, there is a private realm which can be described, but the description is not the same as the experience it describes and is at best an approximation to it. The conditions required for a language to be comprehensible are not the same as the meaning of the utterances in that language. Meaning is not use and use is not meaning.

Probity, intense labour and great ability are not incompatible with ultimate triviality. You cannot find without seeking, perhaps, but you can certainly seek without finding.

---

16 As a young man, I once suffered from breathlessness caused by viral pneumonia. It took me some time to put a name to the experience because I never considered breathlessness as possible in my case. Symptoms were for patients, not for young doctors.

RECONSIDERING JEAN-PAUL SARTRE

SAMUEL HUX

I T WILL SOON BE four decades since Jean-Paul Sartre died (1980, hard to believe!), so it's a bit too late for an obituary—but not too soon for a reconsideration, I don't think, for a novelist-playwright-critic who was, *for a while (!)*, a great philosopher . . . before committing intellectual suicide. Calling an essay a reconsideration usually suggests a kind of positive reappraisal paying respect to the subject, but I confess I am in fact focused almost as much on myself since a significant part of my intellectual life was spent on consideration of Sartre.

I was blown away by his work when I was an undergraduate, double-majoring in literature and philosophy. My introduction was his 1946 essay, "Existentialism is a Humanism," which I found in Walter Kaufmann's great and influential anthology, *Existentialism from Dostoevsky to Sartre* (1956), which inspired me to read his fiction such as *Nausea* (1938), "The

70

Wall" (1939), and *The Age of Reason* (1945); his plays such as *The Flies* (1943) and *No Exit* (1944); and his philosophical texts such as *The Transcendence of the Ego* (1937), and of course and most important, *Being and Nothingness* (1943)—which body of work is what I dare say most general readers have had in mind when they think of Sartre. Literature engagée; choice and responsibility; commitment; authenticity; good faith and bad; "existence precedes essence:" a heady concoction! I had no idea at that time that Sartre was already on the initial steps toward radically modifying—if not quite disowning—the existentialism which made his name. I later wrote a doctoral dissertation which leaned heavily on Sartre; I published several essays directly about him or touching upon him in cultural reviews—all before I finally said "enough." But not until now have I said, in a different tone of voice, *Enough!*

A decade before Jean-Paul Sartre's death, Michel Contat and Michel Rybalka edited the two-volume compendium, *The Writings of Jean-Paul Sartre* (reviewed by yours truly), which included a collection of seldom-published pieces and a year-by-year annotated bibliography, occasional excerpts included, of everything Sartre had written, from novels and plays to philosophical tomes to prefaces and letters to the editor. Because of its breadth, because of its summaries of occasional journalism not normally available to readers outside France, it was a monumental work for scholars—and it was also a monument, one could hardly escape the impression, of the kind normally reserved for writers safely dead.

Sartre's *Between Existentialism and Marxism*, published about the same time, reminded one that the commemoration, although several years early, was still not premature. An essay on "Kierkegaard: The Singular Universal," for instance, an argument that the Dane's thought can survive only when incorporated into the philosophy of historical dialectic, first Hegelian and now Marxist, reminded one that with some fanfare, Sartre had announced the end of his own Existentialism in 1960 in *Critique of Dialectical Reasoning*. Nothing in the writing that followed could be taken as a change of mind. It was clear: he meant it.

Existentialism, Sartre wrote in the *Critique*, is not a philosophy but an ideology. That is, as he defines the latter, it is the work of those who, coming after the "great flowering" of a philosophical system, "cultivate the domain . . . take an inventory . . . erect certain structures there . . . may even bring about certain internal changes; but they still get their nourishment from the living thought of the great dead"—in this case Karl Marx. Existentialism "is a parasitical system living on the margin of Knowledge [i.e. Marxism], which at first it opposed but into which today it seeks to be integrated." Sartre was willing to buy his way in, convinced that Marxism needs the existentialist ideology to provide itself with the clear sense of human subjectivity it lacks—for all its objectivity about broad historical forces—and make possible a convincing philosophical mediation between the praxis of the individual actor, the particularity of the historical moment, and the socio-historical dialectic.

Sartre was always an intellectually and morally obnoxious character (something I was not aware of, or perhaps neglected to notice, in my days of fandom)—limited by his over-confidence, constitutionally unable to distinguish between a conservative and a fascist—the unacknowledged patron saint of political correctness. *But there was a time when he was no sycophant.* So what did it mean, this offering-up and creepy genuflection before Marx? What did it mean about his philosophy all along?

The central image in *what will last* of Sartre's thought is the mutual conflict between the Self and the Other. In *Being and Nothingness*, a man's coming into existence, the rise of human consciousness, was described as a kind of ontological severance, the "nothingness" of the title, a "hole in the heart of being." As a consciousness, *l'être-pour-soi*, being-for-itself, I am different from the rest of Being, which "is what it is," because I am a potentiality. I create my identity day by day; I am a transcendence; I do not have the fixity of a thing, *l'être-en-soi*, being-in-itself. Since a consciousness exists only as a consciousness *of* something, I am a series of "intentions" upon the world about me.

But a part of that world is the Other—who first appears to

me as a thing, *en-soi*; he is after all the *object* of my consciousness. Gradually I notice that he is looking at me, and I assume
correctly that he in turn views me as *en-soi*. The *Look*. He ob-
jectifies me as I do him. Since we are both consciousnesses, "intentions" who need something to "intend" upon, we are mutually dependent. But since at the same time one experiences the
other as something that rejects objectification by returning it,
we experience each other as threats. We each steal the other's
freedom as a non-object; we each refuse to have our freedom
stolen. We are necessary antagonists; our basic relationship is
one of mutual aggression.

That is the most publicized image—or rather, half-image—
in *Being and Nothingness*. Much less acknowledged is Sartre's
fragile resolution of that conflict, his attempt to explain how a
community of purpose can arise between such natural antagonists.

Imagine that I and the Other are experiencing the reciprocal "Look" when an accident occurs in the street and we each
turn to view it. "Immediately," says Sartre, "at the very instant
when I become a spectator of the incident, I experience myself
non-thetically as engaged in 'we.' The earlier rivalries . . . have
(momentarily) disappeared . . . 'We' look at the event, 'we'
take part." Such an experience is fleeting, however. So imagine
another situation. I versus the Other. Suddenly a "Third" appears and looks at . . . Us. To the Third we are "them." We are
converted by the Third's Look into objects—but, as well, into an
incipient collective "which I agree in solidarity with the Other
to constitute. And to the extent that on principle I assume my
being-outside for the Third, I must similarly assume the Other's
being-outside; what I assume is a community of equivalence by
means of which I exist in a form which like the Other I agree to
constitute." Sartre's example of men in the street is only a beginning metaphor, for he has in mind a larger significance for the
Third. It sounds like the *Critique of Dialectical Reasoning*, but
it's still *Being and Nothingness*.

The "master," the "feudal lord," the "bourgeois" (Sartre fan-
cying himself an honorary proletarian), the "capitalist," all of

them "appear not only as powerful people who command but in addition and above all as Thirds; that is, as those who are outside the oppressed community and for whom this community exists. It is therefore for them in their freedom that the reality of the oppressed class is going to exist. They cause it to be born by their look."

The image of I and the Other reappears in the *Critique*: our hostility, our awkward and suspicious movement toward a We—but all, as we will see, on a fundamentally different ground. This image of antagonism and its resolution is, I think, Sartre's major offering to Marxism in the hundreds of pages of the *Critique*, his attempt to give Marxism a believable and non-mechanistic anthropology. But it is also an attempt to show how it is possible to believe in collective action without sacrificing a belief in the antagonistic nature of human beings.

Sartre may be the most significant philosopher of all time to lavish so much attention upon people standing about on street corners. But in the *Critique,* we're waiting for a bus. We already have a relationship of a kind: we are an un-adhesive collection of isolated consciousnesses, *singly* possessing the same goal of gaining a seat. But this requires no more cooperation than our simply standing there in a file. We are a "series" (Sartre calls it); our relationship is merely and casually "seriality." Insofar as we are in a series, and of course there are more momentous series than bus queues—classes, ethnic groupings, and so on, the situations we are born into—we exist, each one for himself, in the *practico-inerte*, Sartre's term for the lumpy, disparate, non-purposive, casual thereness of society, the social residue perhaps of previous purposive orders lapsed into inertia.

While I remain in a series, my eyes set on a private goal—a seat, for instance, or better yet, an adequate wage for some*one* of my class in my society's economy—I am not greatly different from that *l'être-pour-soi* staring about suspiciously at the Others who are merely part of *l'être-en-soi*. But when I recognize, or am made to recognize by external pressures, that the goal I *singly* possess, as do Others in the series, I also share with them, I am on my way toward a mutual agreement to constitute a *group*—

Sartre's word for a series that becomes conscious of its collective power. We take over the bus, as it were, and distribute the seats equitably. Or: We become a revolutionary proletariat instead of a seriality of wage earners. Or: etcetera.

But this "group" was created with much more ease, with much less difficulty in overcoming rivalries within the series, than that "community of equivalence" which I agreed with the Other to constitute back in *Being and Nothingness*. This relative ease is because the Sartre of the *Critique* has changed his mind about what made us antagonists in the first place: Our hostility is not *ontologically* grounded after all; it is not the result of my consciousness being born as a severance between me and all the rest of Being. It is not a matter of the Look. Rather, it is a matter of socio-economics: we are antagonists prior to the constitution of the group because of *scarcity*, because of our conflicting *needs*. Sartre has made his analysis more amenable to the Marxist, but—it seems to me—at the expense of cutting the heart out of his philosophy.

It might be said, on the other hand, that such a cost has its compensation: a much more hopeful and humanistic view of things. But the story is hardly over, for a problem arises that Sartre tries to resolve in a way that will not satisfy those who applaud the hopeful compensation—and which will eventually lead us to the question of authority.

I have already suggested that an element of the *practico-in-erte* is the residue of numerous "groups" that have lapsed into seriality. And, indeed, the problem of the group is that its lasting power is suspect, dependent upon the specific shared project of the constituents. Suppose there is a gain that appears less temporary than it actually is: how can the group remain "fused?" It cannot, forever, unless/until there is no more scarcity, in which case, I suppose, there would be no need. In the meantime, to prevent a rhythm of series and group and group and series, the constituents make an "oath," a kind of contract, and exercise upon any recalcitrant constituent the *terreur*. There has already been something like a Third: people and institutions that benefit from seriality and the nullifying conflict of mine and the Other's rivalrous needs. But now the Terror is a kind of Third, interiorized within the group. There is an improvement of a sort, for collectivity in this scheme is not merely a kind of near-impotent parasitical responsiveness to whatever oppresses us from outside, a dependence upon being oppressed in order to be a group instead of a series; rather, now, we are held together from inside—or seemingly so.

Now while the Terror sounds more terrible in ordinary language than it necessarily does in political thought, where it can suggest the administering of the discipline deemed necessary within a movement, a party, a nation, we should not launder the word too much by ignoring ordinary connotations. We know what Committees of Public Safety are, and revolutionary cadres, and dictatorships of the proletariat. To be fair, Sartre does not play dumb to implications in his analysis. He suggests a certain inevitability to the Bolshevik revolution's remaining "fused" by a combination of "bureaucracy, terror, and personality cult." But I don't think we should be disarmed either by preventive, disarming admissions and mumble something about the necessity of breaking eggs to make omelets.

George Lichtheim was perfectly right: "Sartre's attitude to the Russian Revolution and Stalin is more or less that of Hegel to the French Revolution and Napoleon." And we should take thorough note of how little the individual is considered, compared to the group-in-fusion, to the "Fraternity of Terror," as Sartre calls it with no hint of humor. Lionel Abel once pointed out that a strange reversal from *Being and Nothingness* takes place at this point in the *Critique*. The individual consciousness was, back in 1943, *l'être-pour-soi*, as against the inertness of *l'être-en-soi*; but now in 1960, the group is in effect the *pour-soi*, while the individual consciousness, threatening the dissolution of the "fraternity" into the *practico-inerte*, is the *en-soi*, the mere sodden thereness of Being.

A tentative judgment or two is in order. Sartre's contribution to political thought is shown in the *Critique* to be essentially Hobbesean. Which is no small thing! Except that Sartre's analysis is not so profound as to be the least improvement over

Thomas Hobbes, nor so very haunting and revelatory. One is not inclined to say here as a critic said of Hobbes, "We are not often led to the brink of the abyss and asked to look at ourselves, as in a darkened mirror." Indeed, there is something unconvincing and something pedestrian in being told, as we were not in *Being and Nothingness*, that we are such beasts simply because we are hungry, which is what it amounts to.

But beyond this, I think one really has to question the size of Sartre's fundamental contribution to political sociology. Is his analysis of how groups are formed from antagonistic material reality, to be blunt, beyond the capacities of a moderately talented sociologist? Not that it has to be to be true—but suspicions of a certain hoopla are hard to avoid.

More important, there is no pretense in the *Critique* and Sartre's other "Marxist" (or Marxist-friendly) writings of value-free observation, or even of certain conclusions arrived at with much "sad to say, but . . ." Occasional libertarian rhetoric to the contrary (and there was a great deal of it especially during and after the May "revolution" of 1968), Sartre becomes one of the apologists for a Marxist Leviathan. That's no particular surprise by this time of course, but it is something I should like to approach now in a different and ultimately ironic way.

In the history of Existentialism, where does Max Stirner come in?—asked the English poet and anarchist Sir Herbert Read. Read answered, "Stirner is one of the most existentialist of all past philosophers, and whole pages of *The Ego and His Own* [1848] read like anticipations of Sartre." A consequent meaning of Read's question might be: In the history of anarchism, where does Jean-Paul Sartre come in? Whole pages of *Being and Nothingness* read like resoundings of Stirner. The answer to the second question is: He doesn't, but in many ways he ought to—a fact that makes the totalitarian-friendly position he arrived at all the more perplexing.

Where Sartre *could* have come in is with something like his analysis of the series being fused into a group—something classical anarchism never did succeed in explaining theoretically. How does a singly dissatisfied rebel in *insurrection* against the

oppression of himself come together with other insurrection-
ists to form a *revolution*, which is not a single but a political
act? (The distinction is Stirner's.) Mikhail Bakunin's answer was
really none at all, merely a kind of quasi-Marxist magic: Revo-
lutions "come independently of all will and all conspiracies, and
are always brought on by natural force of circumstance," by "the
spontaneous action of the masses"—which masked Bakunin's
own practical cultivation of those conspiracies of which revo-
lutions are, he said, independent. The question is a pertinent
one because of some facts about anarchist political philosophy
which belie popular assumptions about what the classical anarchists believed about humankind: that the human being was an
altruistic animal, cooperative by nature. In fact, their vision was
quite close to Sartre's in *Being and Nothingness.*

About Stirner there can be no quarrel here. The "Libertarian
Egoist" taught that the individual realizes himself in the "combat of self-assertion" against others, seeing the others as objects,
his own "property." The picture is essentially that of those alien
consciousnesses in *Being and Nothingness* in mutual aggression
against, and objectification of, each other, each realizing himself
in the combat of intentions. But Stirner is usually seen as something of a peripheral figure in the anarchist tradition, finding his
uncomfortable place as the "lonely rhapsodist of the uniqueness
of every human being," as the historian of anarchism, George
Woodcock, put it. I suggest, however, that Stirner's vision is
there at the very center of anarchism.

Natural cooperativeness? There are in fact a few statements
which contradict that impression, an example from Pierre-Jo-
seph Proudhon for instance: "Man is a tyrant or slave by his
own will before he is made tyrant or slave by fortune; the heart
of the proletarian is like that of the rich, a cesspool of babbling
sensuality, a home of filth and hypocrisy . . . The greatest ob-
stacle which equality has to overcome is not the aristocratic
pride of the rich, but rather the undisciplined egoism of the
poor." But such a judgment need be no more than rage and impatience with the overdue revolution. It is best to be attentive to
a definition of human nature that is demanded by a basic tenet

of all classical anarchism—whatever the momentary rages or rhapsodies.

"No authority, no government, even if it be popular government; this is the revolution," stated Proudhon. *Even if it be popular government*, the anarchists consistently warned. To expect the revolutionary idealist to remain honest in power was, said Bakunin, "like squaring the circle, an unattainable ideal." Some such statement (with a distinction between government, "delegation of power," and administration, "delegation of work"— Errico Malatesta) was made by all the classical anarchists. And it is tantamount to saying that power corrupts. But why should it, so absolutely, unless man is by nature an imminently corruptible, native oppressor, not naturally cooperative?

If one wishes to retain the notion of natural cooperativeness while retaining the notion that absolutely anyone is corrupted by power, one has to endow the act of governing with some metaphysical property; government is more than those who govern. But anarchism dismissed this notion as, in Malatesta's words, "a disease . . . called the metaphysical tendency." "For us, government is the aggregate of the governors"—an insight that did not keep him from arguing a page later that should the best gain power, they would become tyrants. Which is either to ascribe to government some metaphysical properties beyond the aggregate of the governors or to subscribe to a none-too-altruistic definition of human nature. So, again, how do these egotistical aggressors come together in collective action such as a revolution or, later, a commune?

It might be argued that there was a kind of "Third" implicit in anarchist analysis: the State itself that oppressed him, her, you, me . . . *us*. But, in fact, one of the basics of anarchist thought was that the State unifies no one except those who rule—sometimes. Its natural function is either atomizing people or keeping them atomized; it cultivates what Sartre would later call *seriality*. What was missing from anarchism as a political theory was a convincing go at the kind of analysis that Sartre did attempt as long ago as *Being and Nothingness*, a theory to bridge between the natural ego and the possibility of collective action, outside the myth of a social contract so abhorrent to anarchism.

The purpose of this excursion into anarchist thought is to question the inevitability of Sartre's neo-Marxism. Was he indeed in the earlier "existentialist" works, as he claimed in the *Critique*, cultivating a domain, taking an inventory, erecting certain structures, all of which are meaningless and merely ideological unless nourished by Marxism? I am not about to suggest that Sartre was really an anarchist instead, only that his earlier writings were perfectly congenial with that school of thought, more so than with Marxism. But is there, although different from inevitability, something like poetic justice to the "conversion?"

It is remarkable in such a profoundly political philosopher as Sartre to find so little convincing concern with *authority*—that mysterious something that "legitimizes" certain behavior and not others. Authority is difficult to explain and resistant to questioning, but is assumed whenever we do more than merely describe an event or course of action. Where is authority in Sartre's scheme, rejecting as he does any transcendental values or any notion that legitimacy derives from the long, deep past? We know better than to expect him to locate authority, as Plato tried to, in the laws, "which are our parents" (*Crito*). Bourgeois parents, Sartre would have answered, and that's that. There is a paucity of vision here, almost amounting to a lack of curiosity in some respects. I will eat a dozen berets if it is ever proven that Sartre so much as glanced at a page of Edmund Burke's *Reflections on the Revolution in France*, the failure of which to consider is intellectually fatal to anyone presuming to write about revolution, whether from the left or the right.

An "authority" he sees no need to rationalize arises for Sartre *ex nihilo* in the praxis of the group fused by a revolutionary project. As long ago as his 1946 essay, "Materialism and Revolution," his first extended critique of Marxism, Sartre argued that since the revolutionary is willing to sacrifice his life—*and others'!*—for a future social order, for the "antiphysis" ("a rational adjustment of human relationships" replacing "what has been produced blindly by nature"), that future then "acts as a value for him," and, "What is a value if not the call of something which does not yet exist?"

Authority is located, then, not in the transcendental realm, or in tradition, but in the *future!* A religious visionary might say something similar, but would mean that the future Holy Commonwealth is a projection of, as it corresponds to, presently held views that derive from a transcendental source—or perhaps is a recovery of the true nature of things, a prelapsarian grace. But not so for Sartre: values are made, not derived or recovered. That future that justifies present action is being created by our acts. Those acts—dependent for their justification upon the future they are creating—are creating the source of their own justification. The end that justifies the means is being created by the means that need justification by the end. This is very tiring, and philosophically suffocating. But accept the magic for the moment.

When the group threatens to lapse into the *practico-inerte,* threatens that is to disintegrate, "authority" resides in the exercise of the Terror. The Terror holds the group together. But if "authority" was originally the call of the future ("something which does not yet exist"), then by what right does the Terror presume to be authoritative when the future stops calling? And that, of course, is what has happened when the group threatens to disintegrate.

Sartre's kind of "authority" doesn't really come into being until the call of values has failed. His position amounts to saying that violence or the threat of violence is authority—which people *are* willing to say. But I rather agree with Hannah Arendt: "Since authority always demands obedience, it is commonly mistaken for some form of power or violence. Yet authority precludes the use of external means of coercion; where force is used, authority itself has failed." What Sartre calls authority, it seems to me, is not authority; rather, it is the failure of authority.

Questions of authority are not academic. For it is a matter of sustaining one's vision amidst choices and decisions. Without some stable sense of authority, one can grow incredibly fatigued—which is what I think happened to Sartre. Consider all he offers us: A Hobbesean vision of humankind, and at the same time, a sentiment (that's all it can be, for it is grounded in no logical necessity) in favor of an *antiphysis* of "popular democratic" ideals; a rejection of transcendental values and all God-talk as sources of authority; a rejection of the mysterious notion that the passage of time can convey a kind of legitimacy (as Nathaniel Hawthorne put it, "custom, so immemorial, that it looks like nature"); and no appeal to human nature itself, since that's the source of the antagonism that creates the difficulty in the first place. All this becomes a burden one escapes by elevating political musculature, by equating authority, makeshift, with force, and then easing one's sensibilities by saying that any broken eggs are necessary for the realization of that sentiment. Moving in circles may become fatiguing—or one may move in circles because one is fatigued. Give me an arm, Saint Vladimir Ilich!

The classical anarchists, subject to similar quandaries deriving from an implicit definition of human nature that could not sustain their ideal of free mutualism, did not tire so thoroughly. The image of the 78-year-old Peter Kropotkin lecturing V.I. Lenin on power and abuse comes to mind. Perhaps the anarchists were philosophically naïve, intellectually too weak to take their presuppositions to the ultimate conclusions, or merely inconsistent. But perhaps, ironically, what one needs is an acceptance of inconsistency, if that's what it is, a willed belief in the meta-empirical, a locating of authority in faith or custom or some such—imperfect perhaps, maybe only a higher or more poetic pragmatism, but more humane than the sad-to-say-but embrace of practical (and ultimately Stalinist) force.

And perhaps the truth is that Sartre was just too bloody consistent . . . about some things. No hankering after authority outside or beyond *the action which works right now at any rate*. Here's the group; take the oath; respect the *terreur*; and let's see. By what authority should you behave in a certain way? By that of the oath you took that is legitimized by the Terror that enforces it. There is no particular difference between Sartre's view of "authority" and a famous saying of Mao to the effect that power comes from the barrel of a gun.

Finally, for all Sartre's proclaimed progressivism, his political imagination is very old-fashioned—but in no particularly remarkable or refreshed way. What is remarkable is how adventurous, thrilling, and even profound one can appear—to tremendous applause—if one depicts the slow, tired descent into Leviathan with revolutionary rhetoric.

(All that said, appealing to Saint Lenin is a classier act than sucking up to New Left student revolutionaries—as I get ahead of myself for a moment.)

Allow me a tactical reminder: Sartre argued in *Critique of Dialectical Reasoning* that Marxism is "the philosophy of our time" which "we cannot go beyond because we have not gone beyond the circumstances which engendered it." Thus, existentialism must remain an "autonomous ideology" until Marxist historical dialectics, lacking the clear grasp of human subjectivity which existentialism has, incorporates this ideology—then "existentialism will no longer have any reason for being." (Too bad, Ex, you can drop dead later.)

A dozen years later, he published *Between Existentialism and Marxism*, as I mentioned much earlier, which in spite of the title suggesting a sustained thesis and sounding like a condition of philosophical death-watch, is not directly about the assumptions of the *Critique*. Or directly about Sartre's humble willingness to self-destruct, although his neo-Marxist ideas do inform it. The book is, rather, a collection of pieces published or republished between the *Critique* and his volumes on Flaubert in 1971-72: four interviews, essays on Vietnam, the Czech repression, Kierkegaard, Mallarmé, Tintoretto, the function of the intellectual, and the transcript of a harrowing, tape-recorded explosion between a fed-up but obviously destructive analysand and his frightened, whining analyst—prefaced by Sartre's Laingian argument for "reciprocity" in the psychoanalytic encounter, with two dissenting evaluations by *Les Temps Moderne* editorial board members.

What provides integrity of a sort to this diversity—as much as the post-*Critique* assumptions do—is a writer's voice and intellectual style I find enormously disappointing.

No matter how abstract the analyses in *Being and Nothing-ness*, the phenomenologist Sartre was able to delineate states of consciousness as well as deep structures of being in almost palpable shape, but Sartre, the philosopher of history, his concerns now more "material," seems to have mislaid that knack for concrete focusing that graced his more "idealist" concerns (as the Marxist called them). *Between Existentialism and Marxism* is too full of explanations like this one of "*le vécu*—lived experience:" "[N]either the precautions of the preconscious, nor the unconscious, nor consciousness, but the terrain in which the individual is perpetually overflowed by himself and his riches and consciousness plays the trick of determining itself by forgetfulness." Enough of this unintended parody of academese and we're liable to forget the Sartre so wonderfully attuned to the world's body and clothing with a perceptual range from *nausea*, as in his first novel (when the "diversity of things, their individuality" vanishes, "leaving soft, monstrous masses, all in disorder—naked, in a frightful obscene nakedness"), to elegant pleasure, as with Calder's mobiles ("a small local festival, an object defined by its movement and nonexistent apart from it, a flower that withers as soon as it stops moving, a free play of movement, like coruscating light").

But the poet of the visual appears occasionally in this book. His Tintoretto piece is a beautiful essay, a rich journey across the face of a painting and into its conception. One is reminded that Sartre was a marvelous art critic, and wonders if that talent had something to do with his abilities as a phenomenologist. Sartre on the Venetian sky which "all [Tintoretto's] work testifies to:" "In Venice the sky shimmers around the pale fingers of the city, crackles drily at eye-level—while up there above the stratosphere it appears as series of loose, grey silken folds receding out of sight. Between this delicate silken scarf and the rooftops there is a void, a wasteland criss-crossed with scintilla of light. Even when the heat is intense, the sun remains 'cool': yet nowhere in the world does it erode so much. It can make an island vanish, disintegrate a district, fall into a canal and evapo-

rate the water, turn the gentle lapping of the waves into a spar-
kling stammer."

But such seeing and writing becomes the exception. More
characteristic are the displays of admitted polemical genius
("when established power," I think he means Western and capitalist power, "judges it useful to tell the truth, it is because it has
no better lie available. Such truth, issuing from official mouths,
becomes no more than a lie corroborated by facts"), and the
kind of blinding obscurity I have mentioned already.

And something else: When Sartre tells an interviewer that
in 1936 or '40-'41 there was no other choice but to go along
with the Communist Party, we can judge that as the familiar
nonsense it is. But in the course of a supposedly rigorous philosophical essay on genocide written for the Bertrand Russell
"War Crimes Tribunal," defining genocide on the grounds of
intent to destroy a race *as a race*, Sartre notes along the way
an American attempt to bribe North Vietnam with economic
assistance, suggests that this would mean the destruction of that
country's socialism, and casually adds, "And that too is genocide." Is Sartre really such a careless thinker, or is this special
pleading disguised as legal philosophy? The disguise doesn't
work. This is disgusting.

Recall his embarrassing defense of the Soviet Union in
the early '50s against charges of imperialism even before his
neo-Marxism. He defends that defense in *Between Existential
and Marxism* not on grounds of truth, but because "it was essential to reject this accusation if one did not wish to find himself on the side of the Americans." I mean this question quite
seriously: Considering that Sartre wrote a play, *Dirty Hands*,
about the question of immoral action in service of an embraced
ideology, is it possible that he had been acting over the years in
re-runs of an unwritten play called *Dirty Thoughts?*

Occasional access to fast and loose standards of honesty
aside, Sartre's collection is a disappointment. I miss the mind
that, in *Being and Nothingness*, taught me why one person can
be so rotten to another. I don't see that the later corrections are
a philosophical advance. Of course, Sartre was under no obli-

gation not to change. But . . . oh my god! I am disturbed at the willingness to emasculate one's thought, to heel contortedly to the moment's revolutionary necessities, so conceived. Sartre announces to a juvenile infantile-leftist interviewer, "Now I consider myself available for any correct political tasks requested of me"—this cringe-provoking moment occured long before anyone knew the phrase "political correctness." To the very end, Sartre still worried himself about being a *bourgeois* leftist intellectual, one of those who in spite of his "political denunciation" of society "remains objectively an enemy of the people" unless he "negate[s] his intellectual moment in order to try to achieve a new *popular* stature." He might have considered—it seems to me—that self-flagellation is one of the more petty bourgeois leftist habits. I prefer looking at paintings, reading poetry, following my better half to the ballet without apologizing, as Sartre does to the interviewer for continuing his *Flaubert*, an interruption of his "correct political tasks." As I said a moment ago, in a slightly different context, this is disgusting.

I never could have thought back in the days of my undergraduate and youngish faculty intellectual love affair with Sartre that I would eventually say "*Enough!*" in an essay that could have been entitled—instead of "Reconsidering Jean-Paul Sartre"—"Thoughts on J.-P. Sartre the Obsequious."

BERTRAND RUSSELL:
WHY RUSSELL WASN'T A CHRISTIAN

KENNETH FRANCIS

THE DISTINGUISHED atheist philosopher, Thomas Nagel, who is admired by many theistic academics, said: "I want atheism to be true and am made uneasy by the fact that some of the most intelligent and well-informed people I know are religious believers. It isn't just that I don't believe in God and, naturally, hope that I'm right in my belief. It's that I hope there is no God! I don't want there to be a God; I don't want the universe to be like that."[1]

This fear of the existence of God was, and still is, no stranger to some atheist philosophers both dead and living. It's also no stranger to psychopaths and moral degenerates. There are various reasons for such emotional fear of a Cosmic Authority. One such philosopher who didn't like the idea of a Cosmic Authority

---

1 Thomas Nagel, *The Last Word*, Oxford University Press, 1997.

was British atheist Bertrand Russell (1872-1970). Russell was an enigmatic man who hated Christianity but had great faith in Naturalism.

He also unquestionably gravitated towards the ideology of scientism: The quasi-religious belief that science can answer everything. One of the problems with such a world-view is it precludes philosophy. And without philosophy, it's quite difficult, if not impossible, to do science. Think about it: In order to make sense of a scientific discovery or theory, we must express such concepts with language and logic, i.e., philosophically. And Russell's philosophical views had many shortcomings.

In an interview with Russell in 1959, the late John Freeman asked him what would be the worst possible thing to happen to mankind. Russell replied that total annihilation of the human race by nuclear war would be the worst possible thing.[2]

This was a strange answer from a man who wasn't a great lover of humanity. And even if he did love his fellow man, what is philosophically strange about this answer is this question: how would anyone know if there were total annihilation of the human race if there would be no one around to know it?

Russell, at the time he was interviewed was regarded by the "intelligentsia" dilettantes, as the world's greatest philosopher; he was not a "Pee-Wee Herman"-type being interviewed by Oprah. And as an atheist philosopher, he should've been aware that his answer was philosophically nonsensical as there would be no human consciousness to lament the aftermath of such an event.

Fans of Russell might argue, "But, as a living human in the here and now, he was commenting on the foreseeable consequences of such a tragedy." I doubt it. Russell was well aware of the second law of thermodynamics. One result of such a scenario is the Earth being incinerated by the sun in the not-so-distant future. Russell even wrote about the endgame of both the Earth's fate and that of the universe, so a nuclear holocaust just puts the clock back a bit before all life perishes with a uni-

---

2   Bertrand Russell – Interview, *Face to Face*, with John Freeman, 1959. https://www.youtube.com/watch?v=a10A5PneXlo (23:50-minute mark).

verse expanding out into the void—a universe in ruins. Such a bleak scenario doesn't bother the Christian, as God ultimately intervenes and we await eternal salvation in the beatific vision.

But Russell was a non-believer and a man of many contradictions. Which brings me to his famous essay, "Why I Am Not a Christian." He delivered the text of his essay on March 6, 1927, at the National Secular Society in London. His reasons for not being a Christian vary, but the crux of his essay is as follows: The Roman Catholic Church is mistaken to say that the existence of God can be proved by unaided reason. Serious defects in the character and teachings of Jesus show that he was not the best and wisest of men, but actually morally inferior to Buddha and Socrates. People accept religion on emotional grounds, particularly on the foundation of fear, which is "not worthy of self-respecting human beings." The Christian religion "has been and still is the principal enemy of moral progress in the world."

Now, before you start accusing Richard Dawkins of plagiarism, Russell's arguments have been doing the rounds for a very, very long time. And that is why New Atheism, which is really Old Atheism with grumpy old men, is now dead in the water. Unlike the old atheism of yesteryear, which had a semblance of respectability, the non-believers among the New Atheists resort to ad hominem attacks coupled with theologically illiterate, unsophisticated arguments.

But back to Russell. He was wrong to argue that Catholicism is based on the blind faith of unaided reason. Had he ever considered the following questions?

- Did he want to lead an immoral life, but God got in the way? Did he want moral autonomy?
- Was the pursuit of happiness, at any cost, his ultimate goal in life? And was it because when he prayed to God, if he ever did, He did not grant him happiness, so he lost his faith?
- Or was it because it was not cool to believe in the God of Christianity, and he became unpopular with his peers by believing in Him? Or the fear that by believing

in exclusive truth, people were offended and ridiculed him for not being "tolerant" or "open-minded?" Did the idea of Sin and Hell put him off believing?

These are just some of the many questions, not just for Russell, but for all those who have lost their faith. For those who still believe in the God of Christianity, but have selected only the parts of scripture that fit in with their world-view, they should also consider the following questions: Is it happiness or Truth that you want? Or:

- Did the other religions in the world make you feel it was arrogant to believe Christianity is the one true religion?
- Did apathy force you to abandon logic and instead be guided by your feelings?
- Did certain "unpleasant" moral obligations in Christianity make you feel bad because you could not live up to them?
- And if something gets in the way of your happiness, does that automatically mean it is untrue?
- Does everything in the Bible have to feel good in order to be true? In other words, if God's rules do not live up to one's expectations, can they be true?
- But didn't Jesus tell us many things that we did not want to hear but needed to hear?

All of these questions leave us with the Ultimate Question: What is the central message in the Bible, the one that comes before all the rest? For this, we must look at the Gospel of John and briefly interpret its meaning:

In the beginning was the Word, and the Word was with God, and the Word was God. The same was in the beginning was God. All things were made by Him, and without Him was made nothing that was made. In Him was life, and the life was the light of men: and the light shineth in darkness, and the darkness did not comprehend it.

What the "Word" seems to mean here is Logic, Reason, God: The universe complete with a Moral Order.

The opening words of the Bible tell us that the universe had a beginning (a "Big Bang"). This means it could not have popped into existence out of something physical. It had to be beyond nature because it created nature. And a Big Bang needs something non-physical, all-powerful and eternal (outside time and space) in order for it to "bang," creating time and space.

Ancient teachings and books prior to the Bible, and even in modern times, claim(ed) the universe is eternal. Russell said the universe was a brute fact. But one of the most reliable facts of science is, as mentioned above, the second law of thermo-dynamics. The consequence of this law is in harmony with the opening lines in Genesis: "In the beginning..." In other words, the observable universe is the result of a "Big Bang," which has since been expanding and gradually running out of energy.

The only candidate for the creation of the universe and cause of this Big Bang of creation, is an uncaused, non-physi-cal, all-powerful eternal Mind, i.e., God. To repeat, for Russell, everything, including the cosmos, is just a big brutal fact, and nothing else.

As we dig deeper into the motivations of Russell, the more we see a God getting in the way of moral autonomy. And Russell was a man who craved moral autonomy, as do his many devoted followers to this day, many of whom are academic scholars and society intellectuals.

What seems to have motivated Russell was not logic or pure reason but what he subjectively felt was right or wrong. But don't take my word for it. In 1948, on BBC Radio, Russell debated the existence of God with the Catholic priest, Fr. Fredrick C. Copleston.[3] When asked about distinguishing between what is good or bad, this is what Russell said in the following Q&A:

Copleston: "...What's your justification for distinguish-ing between good and bad or how do you view the dis-

---

3   Fr. Copleston vs. Bertrand Russell: 1948 *BBC Radio Debate* on the Exis-tence of God.

tinction between them?

Russell: I don't have any justification any more than I have when I distinguish between blue and yellow. What is my justification for distinguishing between blue and yellow? I can see they are different.

Copleston: Well, that is an excellent justification, I agree. You distinguish blue and yellow by seeing them, so you distinguish good and bad by what faculty?

Russell: By my feelings.

So, there you have it readers: For Russell, it's feelings before logic at a time over 60 years ago when the world's college campuses were void of any "snowflakes." It seems Russell accepted his faith of unprovable atheism on emotional grounds. Is it any wonder that he wasn't a Christian?

But, to be fair to Russell, I'd like to conclude on a positive note. Like all of us, there is "Bad Bertrand" and "Good Bertrand." "Good Bertrand Russell" wrote and interesting essay on appearance and reality, which is worth reading, despite it being inspired by the ideas of Plato's Cave and George Berkeley's Idealism.

But it's another quote by Russell that I'd like to end on, as it shows his deep understanding of the ramifications of atheism. In his book, *A Free Man's Worship*, Russell bleakly laments:

> That man is the product of causes which had no prevision of the end they were achieving; that his origin, his growth, his hopes and fears, his loves and his beliefs, are but the outcome of accidental collocations of atoms; that no fire, no heroism, no intensity of thought and feeling, can preserve an individual life beyond the grave; that all the labours of the ages, all the devotion, all the inspiration, all the noonday brightness of human genius, are destined to extinction in the vast death of the solar system, and that the whole temple of Man's achievement must inevitably be buried beneath the debris of a uni-

verse in ruins—all these things, if not quite beyond dispute, are yet so nearly certain, that no philosophy which rejects them can hope to stand. Only within the scaffolding of these truths, only on the firm foundation of unyielding despair, can the soul's habitation henceforth be safely built.

One must commend Russell's profound command of the ramifications of a godless universe. But fortunately, I believe there is a God because something caused the universe and science points to a First Cause. I can only speculate that intellectual pride prevented Russell from believing in this.

JOHN STUART MILL (1806–73)

THEODORE DALRYMPLE

N O ONE WHO HAS SEEN the portrait of John Stuart Mill painted in the last year of his life by G.F. Watts (once known as *England's Michelangelo*) could seriously doubt either Mill's seriousness or his probity. He has the unbending or granitic look of a prophet who has been, and is still, without honour in his own country. Life for him was evidently a hard grind and little else. It would be difficult to lie to him and one would be on one's guard not to say something stupid in front of him. One would probably also avoid jokes. Levity was neither his strong nor his weak point.

Not every philosopher admires Mill. Nietzsche had a special contempt for him but I think underestimated his complexity, both as a man and a thinker. Mill's autobiography, published posthumously in the year of his death, is a moving work, principally on account of his struggle to escape his very strange upbringing by his utilitarian father, James Mill, who seemed to want to turn his son into a kind of erudite calculating machine.

His essay, *On Liberty*, is certainly his most famous or constantly re-read work and has possibly been the most influential tract of political philosophy during the last half of the twentieth century, comparable in importance to Marx and Engels' *Communist Manifesto*. For reasons which I shall indicate, its influence, at least as Mill wanted it to have, is now waning, though it has not entirely dissipated. It has been so important that many people quote him, or his argument, without having read him and therefore without realising that they are doing so.

Mill's purpose is to lay down the extent and limits of freedom in the political sense. (He is not concerned in the essay with the problem of the freedom of the will.) How far may a man decide for himself what to do and how to behave? The most famous passage of his work is undoubtedly the following:

> The object of this Essay is to assert one very simple principle, as entitled to govern absolutely the dealings of society with the individual in the way of compulsion and control, whether the means be physical force in the form of legal penalties, or the coercion of public opinion. That the only purpose for which power can be rightfully exercised over any member of a civilized community against his will, is to prevent harm to others. His own good, either physical or moral, is not a sufficient warrant. He cannot rightfully be compelled to do or to forbear because it will be better for him to do so, because it will make him happier, because, in the opinion of others, to do so would be wise, or even right. These are good reasons for remonstrating with him, or reasoning with him, or persuading him, or entreating him, but not for compelling him, or visiting him with any evil in case he do otherwise. To justify that, the conduct from which it is desired to deter him, must be calculated to produce evil in someone else. The only part of the conduct of any one, for which he is amenable to society, is that which concerns others. In the part which merely concerns himself, his independence is, of right, absolute. Over himself, over his own body and mind, the individual is

sovereign.[1]

Often and often, one hears people saying, in defence of an act that has displeased another, "I was not harming anyone," as if that were a complete defence – as Mill would have that it is.

Before I go any further, I should like to draw attention to Mill's admirable prose. The one thing of which he cannot be accused is trying to obscure his meaning. This is not incompatible with a regard for the importance of rhetoric: his words have a force that survives all criticism of their meaning. For Mill, form was evidently important; his *Autobiography* makes clear his susceptibility to the beauty of language.

Clarity of expression, however, is no guarantee of coherence of doctrine, and beauty of language even less so. Contradictory assertions can be made with perfect clarity. Perhaps the fundamental problem of the essay is its desire to lay down "one very simple principle" to govern the mutual relations of society and individual. Human existence is so complex, and the circumstances of life so infinitely variable, that absolute rules cannot be laid down to cover all possible cases; at best, the rules are guidelines. Any rule that is regarded as absolute fails to recognise that human desiderata are many, not necessarily mutually compatible, and of an importance relative to each other that varies with conditions. The search for a simple principle is the search for a Procrustean bed, as later Mill himself recognised towards the end of the *Essay* when he tries, in the light of his "very simple principle," to delimit the proper scope of governmental action:

> To determine the point at which evils, so formidable to human freedom and advancement, begin, or rather at which point they begin to predominate over the benefits attending the collective application of the force of society… for the removal of the obstacles which stand in the way of the way of its well-being… is one of the most difficult and complicated questions in the art of government. It is, in great measure, a question of detail… and no absolute rule can be laid down.

---

1 I have given no page numbers because editions of On Liberty are so numerous that no readers will have the same one.

But the "very simple principle" is supposed to be precisely such an absolute rule; it has failed to be such only a hundred or a hundred and fifty pages after it was enunciated.

Mill is in difficulty because early on in the *Essay* he has eschewed the assertion that liberty is a good or end in itself:

> It is proper to state that I forgo any advantage which could be derived from the idea of abstract right, as a thing independent of utility. I regard utility [the greatest good of the greatest number] as the ultimate appeal on all ethical questions...

In other words, it has to be proved empirically that, overall, liberty is good for humanity, as measured presumably by aggregate happiness, that the harm it may do some is more than outweighed by the benefits that accrue to humanity as a whole; but according to his "very simple principle," it is never the case that local limitation of freedom can conduce to the overall benefit of mankind because, *ex hypothesi*, it is never justified. But is this really so? Is it even plausible, even were the concept of aggregate happiness to have any possible meaning or application?

By refusing to make liberty an end in itself, Mill falls foul of the warning by his close friend, Tocqueville, that he who seeks in freedom anything but freedom itself is destined for slavery. By making liberty a matter of utility, Mill has to show that each individual suppression of liberty is harmful to humanity as a whole, and it is doubtful whether this could ever be done. On the other hand, of course, those who value liberty in itself, *irrespective* of its actual effects in practice, have to explain why liberty as a value should trump all others, such that no amount of disutility could ever count against its exercise. It is not as if everyone without exception does value liberty, and therefore the virtues of liberty are self-evident and therefore do not have to be argued for. There are many people who find the exercise of free choice very difficult and even threatening. I estimated (very roughly) during my time as a prison doctor that between a quarter and a third of prisoners preferred life in prison, at least for a time, to life outside as free persons. The reasons they gave for doing so boiled down to the lack of freedom in prison. They no longer had to decide very much for themselves; if freedom entailed responsibility, they wanted none of it. In a sense, this was a tribute to their self-knowledge: they knew that given a choice, they always chose the wrong thing, destructive to themselves or to others.

There are other instances that point in the same direction. I once had a conversation with the head of personnel of a very large car factory, which needed to recruit workers for the assembly line. The head of personnel said something that surprised me, but on reflection should not have done. The kind of person the factory was looking for, she said, was the kind of person who was content to do as he was told, even at the cost of complete repetitiveness, for which he would be (by his own lights) well remunerated. The factory searched for people without the least initiative or ambition; it rejected people who displayed the slightest sign of either of those traits. In effect what was wanted was contented robots who would work their hours and go home happy, and such could be found in considerable numbers. Of course, they would be free in their little sphere to indulge in such pastimes as they chose, but in their working life they wanted no freedom whatsoever.

Aldous Huxley, in the preface to the second edition of *Brave New World* published in 1948, said that any government that wanted to establish tyranny would allow freedom in two respects or spheres: sex and the consumption of mind-altering drugs. These two liberties would be more than enough to satisfy most people's thirst for freedom, leaving the governors of the state to dictate all else.

One of the attractions of total institutions, as described by Erving Goffman, is the restriction of choice that they place upon their staff, and hence of the necessity to choose and therefore to think. Imposed routine, while an abomination to some, is deeply comforting to many. The idea that life is, or ought to be, a kind of permanent existential supermarket, in which the manner of spending every minute of every day is, or ought to be, a matter of unrestricted choice freely exercised, is unattractive to many people, especially if along with choice goes responsibility for the consequences of the choices made. The fact is that we don't want to have to think about, and be responsible for, everything in our lives; we are happy to abrogate our freedom in many respects, though in the *Essay*, Mill denies that we have the right to do so.

One of the many problems with Mill's doctrine arises from the concept of *harm*—the harm to others that, according to the doctrine, is the sole justification for the limitation of liberties. What counts as harm is indefinitely expansible, especially in a culture impregnated with the most dubious psychological concepts. Of course, Mill was not to know of this development and cannot be blamed for it; harms were so evident and prevalent in the society in which he lived that he could not have imagined the refinement to which the concept would be subjected; where people were at risk of dying from a simple pin-prick, there was no need to go searching for hypothetical harms; but that does not alter the problem.

Distress, for example, becomes a harm in a society of such safety, unprecedented in human history, that the fragility of human existence was transferred from the physical to the psychological sphere. Even in my childhood, we would still chant "Sticks and stones may break my bones, but words will never hurt me," if anyone insulted us. But with the extension of tertiary education, especially in such subjects as psychology and sociology, words and the distress caused by them came to be regarded as real and present harms.

If people can obtain advantages from feeling distress, they will feel it, at least more acutely than if no such advantages were offered. A good example of how distress claimed as a harm can limit the freedom of expression of others has occurred recently in Britain, at the University of Sussex. A professor of philosophy there, called Kathleen Stock, published a book in which she said what until quite recently would not have needed saying, namely that the biological sex of people at birth cannot be altered, and that therefore a supposedly transsexual woman was not really a woman, and a transsexual man was not really a man, but something different. The truth or otherwise of these assertions (how much of modern intellectual life consists either of stating or denying the obvious or asserting and refuting nonsense!) was not the concern of those who started a campaign against her, claiming that she was actually harming transsexuals by the expression of her opinions. Their distress was the harm, though it was also claimed that her opinions promoted hatred of transsexuals—and though it was demonstrably the case that she had never advocated persecution of them, or even adverse criticism of them *qua* transsexuals. Against this, I suppose, it might be argued that her opinions promoted such hatred whether or not they were intended to do so: they did so *objectively*, in the old Stalinist sense, as a matter of sociological or psychological fact.

Mill, I think, would have laughed such claims out of court. He would have said that mere distress at someone's opinion was not to count as a harm, that in a free society people had to swallow such distress, which is an emotion that is self-reinforcing. His contempt for the Sussex University student, clearly of the middle class, holding up, apparently in all earnestness, a placard saying, "We were meant to be safe here," would have been withering. Professor Stock's book and opinions as a threat to anyone's safety? Fragility, thy name is student! Such fragility is possible only in people who know nothing, have experienced nothing, wish to learn nothing, are without imagination, and who wallow psychologically in a warm bath of self-pity.

To regard exposure to opinions other than one's own as a real harm or danger is a blackmailer's charter. In the famous English children's book, *Just William*, the awful lisping little girl, Violet Elizabeth, says when crossed, "I'll thcream and thcream and thcream until I'm thick. I can!" Since to vomit is an unpleasant and sometimes even dangerous experience, and since she would not have screamed or vomited without provocation, the person who crossed her can be held responsible for harm done to her. This, at any rate, is now an argument taken seriously, for example by the feminist legal theorist, Catherine A. McKinnon, who published *Only Words* nearly thirty years ago, a classic work of what might be called the Violet Elizabeth school of jurisprudence.

I am not sure whether it follows in strict logic that if words can do good they can also do harm, though it seems to me very likely as an empirical fact if not as a logical deduction. Certainly, the law both of incitement and provocation recognises this. But the avoidance of harm can be made the excuse of failure to do anything: there are few inventions, for example, that cannot be turned to ill-purposes. However, without a deontological commitment to freedom, including but not only to freedom of speech, it is difficult to see how Mill's "one very simple principle" could be preserved. I doubt it could be shown that the harm from each and every prohibition of expression, considered separately, did harm to the greatest number, though Mill obviously goes in for a rule type of utilitarianism, which involves the claim that it is better, overall, that a rule should be obeyed than that individual exceptions should be allowed, even if they do a little local harm. But this, surely, cannot merely be asserted, but has to be shown empirically.

Mill tells us that the suppression of any opinion is unjustified for a number of reasons. However unpopular or seemingly absurd, it may yet turn out to be the truth. Even if it does not, it will sharpen the wits of those who hold the contrary opinion who will be put to the trouble of refuting it and thereby coming to know the evidence in favour of their own opinion. Without such exercise of the intellectual muscles, as it were, we will grow mentally flabby or torpid.

Is this an accurate portrayal of the human situation? Most of what we believe is believed on authority, not on an examination of the evidence. This is so even for the most learned person, who cannot be expected to provide a demonstration for all that he believes. How many people in the street could demonstrate that the earth goes round the sun, that there are blood groups, that there was a battle in Hastings in 1066, that Mount Everest is the highest mountain in the world, and that material is composed of atoms and molecules—each and every one of these assertions, let alone the many others that they believe? Would it not be a colossal waste of time and effort, to say nothing of the sheer unpleasantness, if everyone had to defend everything he believed by reference to indisputable evidence? Just think of what would be involved to prove that the Battle of Hastings actually took place, without resort to the authority of historians.

This is not the point, Mill would no doubt retort. Suppose someone were to deny that there had ever been such a battle: would any harm result for such a proposition? While the suppression would be an undoubted harm in itself, most people would at least agree that the default position should be in favour of liberty.

The example is an innocuous one, but not all examples are quite as innocuous. Let us take the criminalisation of Holocaust denial in Austria, which violates Mill's "very simple principle." No one would deny that there are good and obvious reasons for Austria to be especially sensitive on this subject. While we may think that such a law does, on balance, more harm than good, few would deny that it is a difficult case. Although Austria claims to have been one of the first international victims of Nazism, most people know that it was more complicit with Nazism than resistant to it. By banning open expression of Holocaust denial, the Austrian government is, in effect, taking a vote of no confidence in its own people: it is a recognition that the old demons persist, all the more so since there is now in the country a minority population, eight per cent and growing, that is especially susceptible to anti-Semitism, namely the Moslem population. There is surely something to be said on both sides of the question as to the practical effect of the prohibition of Holocaust denial. On the one hand, the prohibition may be taken by the susceptible—a significant portion of the population—as evidence that the government is frightened of the "truth," and what is driven underground often, or sometimes, becomes the stronger for having been subterranean; on the other, to allow propaganda of a false and vicious belief with possible doleful practical consequences would be negligent almost to the point of complicity. It is difficult to say for sure which of these two alternatives is the more true to life: and if the second were, would anyone nevertheless hold to Mill's "very simple principle" in this case?

It is not, alas, difficult to think of other, similar cases. In fact, if Mill were alive and asked today whether he thought the Austrian government was justified in its prohibition of public expressions of Holocaust denial, he might well have replied in the affirmative, though this is not certain. As he says in *On Liberty*:

> It is, perhaps, hardly necessary to say that this doctrine is meant to apply only to human beings in the maturity of their faculties... For [this] reason, we may leave out of consideration those backward states of society in which the race itself may be considered in its nonage... Despotism is a legitimate mode of government in dealing with barbarians, provided the end be their improvement, and the means justified by actually effecting that end.[2]

Who has the authority, and based upon what, to decide that a race (by which Mill, I think, means any politically recognisable agglomeration of people rather than what is meant by racists and anti-racists alike) is in its nonage and consequently in a state of backwardness that makes the exercise of liberty either impossible or inadvisable for them? Is one either a barbarian or not? And does barbarism qualify a people as barbarian, and thus make despotism a suitable mode, perhaps the suitable mode, of government for them? If a tendency to barbarism qualifies a population as barbarian, what proportion of the population has to exhibit it before the population itself is deemed barbarian? Do we believe that *barbarian is as barbarian does*? In which case, which population could not be, at least in part, classified as such?

If circumstances alter cases, the "very simple principle" cannot be so very simple after all. Indeed, a case might be made that a people is qualified for liberty in proportion to the simplicity of its society, for in a simple society, all, or a very high proportion

---

2 Compare this with Macaulay's famous dictum, "Many politicians are in the habit of laying it down as a self-evident proposition, that no people ought to be free till they are fit to use their freedom. The maxim is worthy of the fool in the old story, who resolved not to go into the water till he had learned to swim."

of, political decisions not only affect its members directly, but fall within the compass of their understanding. How, by contrast, am I qualified to decide the permissible limits of sulphur dioxide in the ambient air, or whether a new additive to food is likewise permissible, or whether turbines to capture the energy of the tides are viable as a source of energy? If the right to liberty depends upon qualification for it, I am unqualified to express an opinion on most subjects—despite which I persist in maintaining my right to have such an opinion.

The case of the Austrian prohibition of public Holocaust denial illustrates a tension in moral philosophy between deontological and consequentialist principle. A principle is not worth very much if it cannot withstand any adverse consequences whatsoever, however slight or infrequent; on the other hand, a principle which is adhered to whatever its practical consequences becomes a fetish for fanatics. Few people never think in a utilitarian way, but few people always do so. For example, one can easily imagine a scenario in which it was advantageous to society to execute an innocent man, but we should still revolt against doing so.

By making the impermissibility of harm to others the touchstone of his limits to liberty, Mill opens the door to tyranny. In a passage less frequently quoted than the first I have used, for reasons that, in the modern world, are only too obvious, Mill says:

> ... [I]f from idleness or from any other avoidable cause, a man fails to perform his legal duties, as for instance to support his children, it is no tyranny to force him to fulfil this obligation, by compulsory labour, if no other means are available.

Inside every libertarian there is a martinet trying to get out.

The problem with harm to others as a criterion of permissible liberty is that harm is on a continuum, from trivial but still discernible to severe and obvious at first glance. A father may harm his children without starving them to death: he may bully or terrify them; he may refuse them affection. There is conduct that may harm some children and fortify others. Who is to decide what harmful conduct actually is? There have been philosophers recently who considered that a religious upbringing is a form of abuse in itself—as on occasion, no doubt, it can be. The "very simple principle" is evidently rather complex: where the line as to what is counted to be harm that justifies intervention of the state or other actors is drawn is matter of judgment, not an either/or decision.

Mill intends to apply the principle only to that conduct which is principally or overwhelmingly self-regarding. But here again the problem of the continuum raises its head. It is true that we make a rough and ready distinction between those actions which are one's own business and those which are not, but the more closely you look at the distinction, the more problems you see with it.

Perhaps presciently, Mill deals with the question of drugs. Mill objects to the Chinese prohibition on the importation of opium because "the object of the interference is to make it impossible or difficult to obtain a particular commodity." This, in Mill's view, is objectionable, "not as infringement on the liberty of the producer or seller, but that of the buyer."[3]

Let us examine the case of smoking as a test. The harms done by smoking fall most heavily on the person who smokes, of course, and therefore might seem at first to fulfil Mill's criterion for the "sphere of action in which society, as distinguished from the individual, has, if any, only an indirect interest…" This sphere comprehends "all that portion of a person's life and conduct which affects only himself, or if it also affects others, only with their free, voluntary, and undeceived participation."

Evidence suggests that the smoke of others is harmful, in-

---

3   Mill was, until his retirement, an important official - in effect, second in command - of the East India Company, which had a monopoly of the purchase and the export of Indian opium for the Chinese market. I hesitate to say of a man of Mill's integrity that his opinions on the question were but a rationalisation of his practice or self-interest, but the coincidence is unfortunate. At least Mill does not make the mistake of claiming that the choice of the Chinese opium smoker was not a choice at all, and that he was a "slave" to the drug and could therefore do no other than he did. For the reasons why the metaphor of slavery to opium, opiates and opioids is misleading, wilfully so, see my *Romancing Opiates* (*Junk Medicine* in the British edition).

cluding to a smoker's children, who have no say in whether their parents smoke or not. The involuntary exposure to smoke occurs also when it is permitted in public places. The unpleasantness of such exposure, if not the harm done by it, increases as smoking becomes less and less prevalent. When I was growing up, three quarters of adult males smoked, and I do not remember being inconvenienced, let alone repelled, by what must have been the impregnation of practically everything with the disagreeable smell of stale tobacco smoke; but now a single cigarette smoked at a distance on an outdoor terrace is sufficient to make me cough. In my experience, smokers have difficulty in believing that their habit is truly unpleasant to others and that those who complain about it are anything other than zealots rather than people who are being exposed to something disagreeable and noxious.[4]

Even the concept of "free, undeceived and voluntary participation" is not without its complications—and bear in mind once again that Mill was in search of a very simple principle to delimit freedom and control. The late Christopher Hitchens, an ardent smoker, once recounted that after the ban on smoking in public places in New York (a ban with which he disagreed, though in his youth and early adulthood he had been an equally ardent totalitarian), he was determined to break the law, both because he wanted to smoke and as a kind of protest. He was in a restaurant and asked the people at the table next to his whether they minded if he smoked. They said they did not, and therefore Mr. Hitchens concluded that when he lit up, it was with their "free, undeceived and voluntary participation." After all, practically everybody now knows that cigarette smoke is bad for the health. (In nearly fifty years as a doctor, I have never met anyone who didn't know that smoking was bad for the health or that nicotine was addictive, rendering absurd and corrupt the legal proceedings against tobacco companies, however nefarious they may have been.) Exposure to the smoke of a single cigarette is unlikely to have a measurable effect on anybody's life

---

4 When smoking was banned in pubs in Scotland, the rate of heart attacks declined markedly. This is unlikely to be a case of *post hoc, ergo propter hoc*.

expectancy—never mind that one of Mr Hitchens' objects was to make it possible once more for smokers to expose others to their smoke. And since he asked the permission of the people at the table next his for their agreement, he could have claimed, and in fact did claim, that he smoked with their "free, unde-ceived and voluntary participation."

This implies a very crude view of social relations and the use of language to express wishes. Mr. Hitchens failed to real-ise, through egotism or through a desire not to understand, that the question "Do you mind if I smoke?" in the circumstances described is not a neutral one. While it is easy to say "No," it is difficult to say "Yes" in answer to the question. In some sense, then, his question had an element of bullying: "I challenge you to deny me what I want and to give reasons for it." To that ex-tent, the desired answer was required and mildly coerced.

Most of us are willing, on occasion, to put up with inconve-niences and even dangers for the sake of smooth social reasons, to say nothing of our tendency to pusillanimity, into which the desire to be polite sometimes slides. The difference between what counts as "free, undeceived and voluntary participation" on the one hand, and as coercion on the other, is, like many such differences, on a continuum, in which extremes are easy to recognise but in which there are cases difficult to decide. The law requires that there be categorical differences, but reality is something else: which is why law must always allow for mitigat-ing circumstances if it is to retain some connection to justice, and one of the reasons why summary justice is wrong.

Once again, the "very simple principle" turns out not to be so very simple.

Does the reduction in the pleasure of the diners next to Mr. Hitchens in the restaurant as a consequence of his smoking a cigarette (assuming that there was such a reduction) count as a harm, in Mill's sense, and does the pleasure of Mr. Hitchens both in the cigarette and the flouting of the law with which he disagrees weigh against it, and if so, to what extent? The intensi-ty of his pleasure might be greater than the intensity of the dis-pleasure of his fellow diners (or, of course, vice versa). Is there, indeed, a common measure of pleasure and displeasure that would make a utilitarian decision, of the kind required by Mill, even possible? Is any harm whatsoever done to others sufficient to limit a freedom otherwise to be enjoyed? Does the harm have to be actual or only potential? I do not see how the need for judgment can ever be avoided, and insofar as Mill's "very simple principle" is designed to preserve us from the necessity of judgment, which is always intellectually messy, by giving us a tool to decide with which to make indisputable decisions, I think it fails: as, in fact, any such attempt must fail.

Nietzsche despised Mill, thinking him shallow because tepid, or tepid because shallow, but in fact had at least two things in common with him, the first biographical and the second doctrinal. Both men advocated a certain wildness, Dionysian in Nietzsche's case and existentially experimental in Mill's: yet, no man could have been less Dionysian than Nietzsche, and no man could have been less experimental in the way he lived than Mill. True, Mill's relationship with the woman who was to become his wife, Harriet Taylor, was long suspected to have been illicit by Victorian standards, but Mill was very careful to provide no strict evidence for gossips.[5] Mill was perhaps too much a man of his time to be able to imagine where the "experiments in living" which he advocated might lead; in any case, both he and Nietzsche were hardly examples of men living their dreams.

Both men were strong advocates of elitism: they did not believe that every person could contribute equally to life. It is true that Mill's elitism was tepid by comparison with Nietzsche's red in tooth and claw variety, and Mill would never have thought that the existence of a single Napoleon could justify a million deaths. On the contrary, he believed that an intellectual and cultural elite was necessary to promote the greater welfare of the rest of humanity, with which Nietzsche was hardly concerned and of which he was contemptuous. But the fact remains that both believed in the vital importance of tiny minorities.

---

5 His dedication to his recently deceased wife in *On Liberty* is almost nauseating in its fulsomeness and makes eighteenth century dedications to aristocratic patrons seem almost like essays in criticism.

In criticising Mill, I do not mean to disparage him. He tried to do what I think no man can do, that is to say find an indubitable fundamental principle by which to live. I am reminded of what F.H. Bradley said about metaphysics:

> Metaphysics is the finding of bad reasons for what we believe upon instinct; but to find these reasons is no less an instinct.

Though the task of finding indubitable principles by which to live is a hopeless one, human beings above a certain level of economic and intellectual development are impelled, as if by instinct, to devote some effort to the search for such principles. It is like an intermittent itch which cannot be altogether ignored.

Though somewhat at a tangent to the main theme of his tract, Mill devotes some brilliant pages at its end to something more evident today than it was in his own time, namely the tendency of government and bureaucracies to grow in power and scope, which he regards as a threat to liberty. He seems almost to be describing our present predicament:

> Every function superadded to those already exercised by the government, causes its influence over hopes and fears to be more widely diffused, and converts, more and more, the active and ambitious part of the public into hangers-on of the government, or of some party which aims at becoming the government... if the employees of all... enterprises... looked to government for every rise in life; not all the freedom of the press and popular constitution of the legislature would make this or any other country free otherwise than in name.

Mill provides an explanation of why so many reflective people now feel that the ship of state is like a rudderless oil tanker drifting irresistibly (or unresistingly) onto the rocks, change of direction having become impossible:

> To be admitted into the ranks of this bureaucracy,[6] and

---

6 Here it should be added that giant corporations, often dependent on favours of the government—and vice versa—are likewise bureaucracies rather

when admitted to rise therein, would be the sole objects of ambition. Under this régime, not only is the outside public ill-qualified, for want of practical experience, to criticize or check the mode of operation of the bureaucracy, but even if the accidents of despotic or the natural working of popular institutions occasionally rise to the summit no reform that is contrary to the interest of the bureaucracy can be effected. Such is the melancholy condition of the Russian empire... The Czar himself is powerless against the bureaucratic body; he can send any one of them to Siberia, but he cannot govern without them, or against their will. On every decree of his they have a tacit veto, by merely refraining from carrying it into effect... For the governors are as much the slaves of their organization, as the governed are of the governors... the official body are under the constant temptation of sinking into indolent routine, or, if they now and then desert the mill-horse round, of rushing into some half-examined crudity which has struck the fancy of some leading member of the corps...

If, in addition, those admitted to the ranks of the bureaucracy have been subjected to the influence of the long march through the institutions, the results are easily imagined.

With Mill's one simple principle, we can easily see why and how, in the words of Shigalyov, starting from unlimited freedom, we arrive at unlimited despotism.

---

than the entrepreneurial entities often imagined.

JONATHAN EDWARDS
AND THE MORAL ACTION OF THE DAMNED

SAMUEL HUX

WILLIAM JAMES JUST POSSIBLY excepted, the richest, subtlest, and most rewarding thinker ever to grace America was Jonathan Edwards. It's often thought unfortunate that the reading public knows him primarily, when it recalls its lessons, through his sermon, "Sinners in the Hands of an Angry God," instead of the kindlier mood of *A Treatise Concerning Religious Affections* or *Concerning the End for Which God Created the World*, which show him in a better light as psychologist and metaphysician, or *Images or Shadows of Divine Things*, brief essays in analogy which reveal the poet. But the poet is revealed in "Sinners" as well: "The bow of God's wrath is bent, and the arrow made ready on the string, and justice bends the arrow at your heart, and strains the bow, and it is nothing but the mere pleasure of God, and that of an angry God, without any promise or obligation at all, that keeps the arrow one moment from being made drunk with your blood." I cannot think it unfortunate if the popularity or notoriety of this sermon reminds us that at bottom of Edwards' thought, most of which is truly elegant, is an image of man as a poor forked thing, life as a terrifying trial, and the chance of something graceful being done with it hedged by risk and uncertainty and poor material. It could have been Edwards who said, instead of Immanuel Kant (*Idea for a Universal History*), "From such crooked wood as man is made of, nothing perfectly straight can be built."

But the work of Edwards which concerns me most here is his posthumously published *The Nature of True Virtue* (1765)—which is something like his Ethics.

An approbation of justice in human dealings is indisputably a fine thing. But, Edwards argues, it is no evidence in itself of True Virtue, because there is no benevolence necessarily implied. What functions instead is a conventional sense of symmetry not different in kind from what leads us to appreciate proportion in physical things. A man does ill, and has ill done to him; or, a man "promotes the good of another [and] has his good promoted by the other." An observer can appreciate "some natural agreement of one thing to another; some adaptedness of the agent to the object; some answerableness of the act to the occasion; some equality and proportion in things of a similar nature."

A man does ill to another and suffers pangs of conscience. But this is no evidence of True Virtue, no mark of an innate moral sense. It is a matter of "natural conscience," as Edwards calls it, which is a disposition against being inconsistent with oneself, such inconsistency occurring when one treats another in a way he would not want to be treated himself or demands from another a behavior he would not be willing to practice himself.

Love and consideration of one's partner or one's children is clearly admirable. But of itself it is no evidence of True Virtue.

The inclination is a "natural instinct" implanted by the "Author of Nature" for "the preservation or continuation of the world of mankind." Nor is pity for the suffering of a fellow necessarily Truly Virtuous, being another natural instinct implanted for the same purpose. And in fact pity "may consist with true malevolence," as when a person hates another and wishes him ill, but his hatred not being infinite, he begins to pity the other when the other is "in misery far beyond his ill will."

The principles of conduct behind these selective and representative examples Kant (who wrote his *Observations on the Feeling of the Beautiful and Sublime* at about the same time) would have called "adoptive virtues." Such virtues, although praiseworthy and even beautiful, are not sublime ("true virtue alone is sublime"), because while they may accord with true virtue, they do so only incidentally, and indeed may—as Edwards' example of pity suggests—"conflict with the general rules of virtue." If a person feels sympathy for a particular fellow *because* of that particular fellow, the virtue is "adoptive." If he feels sympathy for the particular fellow because he has a universal sympathy, the virtue is "true." This is Edwards' point as well.

Acts or feelings motivated by a sense of proportion, by natural conscience, or by natural instinct are actuated in various degrees by self-love, self-interest. True Virtue is absolutely, disinterestedly benevolent. It has only incidentally to do with a particular other or with any benefits accruing to the self, except in so far as the other and one's self are parts of the all toward which the Truly Virtuous is well disposed.

True Virtue is "benevolence to being in general. Or perhaps, to speak more accurately, it is that consent, propensity and union of heart to being in general;" it is that excellence which "is in the sacred scriptures called by the name of light, knowledge, understanding." What Edwards calls "True Virtue" in *The Nature of True Virtue* he calls by other names in other works. But whatever he calls it, it is the possession only of the one who is Elect. In *A Divine and Supernatural Light*, Edwards pursues the understanding of "a spiritual and divine light, immediately imparted to the soul by God, of a different nature from any that is obtained by natural means"—that is, not the natural instincts and conscience, but True Virtue—the gift of Grace. The adoptive virtues (Kant's term is handier) are meant to pale in comparison.

But. . . may there not be a sense in which the adoptive virtues are *enough?*

A stable polity could be built upon their exercise. It's not a major consideration in Edwards' dissertation (he's not writing a *Politics*), but the pleasure he finds men taking in "a beauty of order in society" is the work of that sense of aesthetic proportion. And the self-love inherent in those natural instincts for human preservation and the self-union inherent in that natural conscience for personal consistency obviously all have a social function. The self-love of natural man is a mark of his fallenness, but a social polity, even a just one, does not depend upon an innate benevolence. Edwards was in part speaking to the philosophers of the Scottish Enlightenment, like Francis Hutcheson, who argues in *An Inquiry into the Original of Our Ideas of Beauty and Virtue* for a native sense of communal benevolence, an innate disinterestedness. Edwards admired Hutcheson, as he makes perfectly clear, but not to the point of saying that the rare gift of a few is the innate propensity of all. In an earthly kingdom, men will have to do with the natural capacities of the vast majority of humankind and trust that apparent concern for others which is actually a reflected solicitude for one's own pains and pleasures.

Nature. Natural conscience. *Natural* instincts. It is well to remind ourselves what "natural" meant to the *Calvinist* Edwards: the state of human existence untouched by Grace. "Natural" is the state of the person who is not Elect. The state of the *Damned.* And all those adoptive virtues that Edwards approves, while finding them to fall far short of True Virtue, inform the social psychology of the Damned—although he's kind enough not to put it that way. True Virtue belongs only to the Elect, God's chosen, the minuscule number seized by Grace.

Yet . . . now . . . considering all this, Edwards' treatise may be a remarkable gesture of benevolence! Consider: This unrelenting Calvinist, who believed—if the famous sermon is anything to go by—that God despised the non-Elect, nevertheless could perform the act of True Virtue that *The Nature of True Virtue* is, and *give to the damned the credit for the greater part of the moral action of the world.*

Read Calvin. Then read Edwards. Ice and fire. Or, rather, the difference between an icy moralism relieved only by the technical requirement of Christian mercy and a warmth deriving from sympathetic closeness to those who will feel the flames, or, as Robert Lowell put it in his magnificent poem on Edwards, those whose souls "full of burning . . . will whistle on a brick."

So, my tribute to Jonathan Edwards is in partial appreciation of his kindness to me. But I'm after some things a great deal more consequential than the opportunity to praise a man I greatly admire.

True Virtue, disinterested benevolence toward being in general, cannot be understood simply as a high, transcendent mode of the ethical. If one treats one's neighbor with respect and sympathy because one is graced with respect and sympathy toward being in general, it is the latter disposition which marks one as Truly Virtuous, not the specific act, which could be performed from lesser motives, the adoptive virtues. Furthermore, in a sense, True Virtue need not be understood as a mode of the ethical in any primary way at all. *The Nature of True Virtue* is, as I put it before, "something like" Edwards' Ethics. An emphasis he gives there to benevolence to being in general is toward human being in general; but it's hardly an exclusive emphasis. Even in that work, True Virtue "must chiefly consist in love to God; the Being of beings, infinitely the greatest and best." In *A Divine and Supernatural Light,* this gift to the Elect is a sense which "acts in the mind of a saint [an Elected one] as an indwelling principle" and—no revolutionary theological faculty revealing new doctrine, no source for opinions—compels one to love of God's word and creation, "the loveliness and beauty of that holiness and grace."

Edwards can barely contain his aesthetic passion. "It struck me—every Day— / The Lightning was as new / As if the Cloud that instant slit / And let the Fire through," or any number of

Emily Dickinson lines. And that's a clue; for ultimately the gift to the Elect is a kind of *talent* for appreciative perceptiveness which some, because they are eloquent, reveal without particularly knowing that that's what they are doing.

The point is essential. For Edwards *put ethics in its place*—a high place, yes, but not so difficult a climb. It's as if Edwards had said: Let us be truthful, see what we have, and judge what is required. There is nothing so mysterious, so defiant of human comprehension, about right action. The common sense which belongs to the self you love so dearly can tell you that if you steal, you're liable to be stolen from and be left with no grounds for objecting; that if you attack, you invite revenge. It may be hard for you to control your greed and aggression; but that it is to your advantage to do so, and to applaud the other for doing so, is easily within your mental grasp. You may be cursed with depravity; you are also blessed with reason and some instincts of preservation. I do not pretend that social comity is easy—I of all people, who have preached man's distance from the angelic—but I note a certain intellectual clarity of alternatives. . . .

Well, few of us are Calvinists today, but many fragments of Calvinist doctrine lie submerged in the assumptions and rhetoric of many of us (a confession?) all the same. One doesn't have to profess Calvinism (or any religious faith for that matter) to ponder the cogency of the words *Elect* and *Damned*—for in some fundamental way they are right. Most of us, let's face it, are not inspired people—whether "inspiration" is read as a religious state of being or just some secular quality of moral and aesthetic excellence. The inspired among us are as few as the Elect in Edwards' reckoning, in which "of so vast and innumerable a multitude of blossoms that appear on a tree, so few come to ripe fruit . . . but one in a great multitude ever bringing forth anything" (*Images or Shadows of Divine Things*).

I can imagine someone protesting, as I would on the other end of a book: Does the writer think that he is one of the Elect / Inspired? I sincerely don't. But that's no adequate answer. For if I did, I would probably for diplomatic reasons not wish to admit that I did. So one will have to judge the author's argument, not guess at his possible delusions. But I recognize the justice of suspicion here—so universal is the habit of self-election!

When Calvin proposed in his *Institutio Christianae Religionis* that among those to whom God assigns Election there are a few to whom he "assigns it in such a manner, that the certainty of the effect is liable to no suspense or doubt," one cannot help thinking that his proposition was really a self-interested self-compliment. And it seems to me that there are many among us who think their own presumptive inspired state, their election so to speak, "is liable to no suspense or doubt." They tend to be people of economic means, social position, or mental capacities beyond the average. I am reminded of Edwards' caveat in *A Divine and Supernatural Light* that special condition knows no distinctions of rank and intellect and may belong to "persons of mean capacities and advantages, as well as those that are of the greatest parts and learning." It's too easy to forget, as Calvinists often did forget, that Calvinism is not a class doctrine.

Not a class doctrine—and, as a matter of fact, of remarkably little political significance at all, in spite of the fact that *Elect* and *Damned* in a secular context do have a suspiciously political sound, the first especially. For you don't say to elect in Basel, where Calvin wrote his *Institutes*, or in Geneva, where he ruled, but *élire*, from which we get *élite*.

That's an icy word as adapted into English, *elite*. It's the possession of the self-assured, those as alien to humility as Calvin was when he overruled the Augustinian doctrine that the mystery of election and damnation took place in God's "secret counsel" and supposed himself privy to the divine knowledge. Such self-assurance, self-election, is rarely conducive of respect for others one suspects of a lesser condition. I haven't any doubt that Edwards in his secret heart assumed himself Elect, but he didn't give up as easily as Calvin did "Augustine's agnosticism about the souls of other men" and thus could manage some humility and sympathy.

That phrase belongs to Garry Wills's reading of Augustine (who strikes many Protestants, anachronistically, as a sort of eloquent Roman Calvinist). In his *Confessions of a Conservative,*

Wills reads Augustine's *The City of God* (Book XIX especially), thus:

Between the City of God (Heaven, Jerusalem, etc.) and the Earthly City (Hell, Babylon, etc.), there is a third city implied, the (no caps) "earthly city." The Heavenly City of God and the Satanic Earthly City are ultimate revelations, destinations. But our earthly order, "the earthly city," is neither the home of perfect justice nor perfect injustice but is rather "that place where the two final cities mingle in pilgrimage" toward their ultimate revelations. In the meantime, while final Cities mingle in our own, the blessed and the cursed among us suffer/enjoy a democracy of need. "Peaceful union is the nutrient, as it were, for both wheat and weeds. By ordaining that both need the same things, God ordained a unity of goal and co-operation between them. His fields nurture both wheat and weeds, till harvest." There can be no perfect injustice here, for while that would reign in the Earthly City in the form of a self-love that is other-hatred, in "the earthly city" there is a "people," which Augustine defines as a "gathering of many rational individuals united by accord on loved things held in common." Nor can there be perfect justice here, for that "accord"—the virtue of peace—may compromise absolute justice. And besides, who is fit to impose even a facsimile of absolute justice here on this earth since no one can be certain that he is blessed with Grace, or that you are not, or that either can remain of a certainty blessed? "Augustine's agnosticism about the souls of other men."

Well . . . we know who can be certain: those who are sure they are the *wheat*, the Elite assuming their Election.

But *Elite* and *Elect* have no relation beyond the coincidence of etymology. Elites have ruled us in politics as often as in fashion. But the Elect never has (although Plato wished it). Elite is always plural, a collective phenomenon. Elect implies the singular, as does *Inspired*. (The religious term is so much the more elegant; allow me to appropriate it even in a secular context.) The Elite are visible and obvious, possessing whatever qualities a society admires and likes to reward or possessing whatever power a society will heel to. The Elect tends to be invisible, for his or her virtues are not cashable. Elites choose, or are allowed to choose, themselves. The Elect is chosen by no one, but simply is. Elitism is a compromise between autocratic impulses and the reality of mass society. The Elect may be a hidden member of that mass. He's of no direct political consequence: how are you going to find him to crown him? But shall we at least make an effort at location?

I need to avoid misleading associations, even with ideas for which I have some sympathy and figures for whom I have some admiration. Aristotle's "high-minded man" of the *Nicomachean Ethics* (IV, 3), given to large risks and concerned with honors, from whom goodness seems to flow because he is actually high-minded rather than his appearing high-minded simply because he is good, a certain deserved haughtiness and singularity. Which character reminds one of the sublime man sought in *Toward a Genealogy of Morals, Thus Spoke Zarathustra, Beyond Good and Evil,* disdainful of characterological weakness, servility of soul, and petty ressentiments, and for whom "good" means "noble" and "bad" means "contemptible," and who rather than subscribing to society's standards is "value-creating" because his actions have the quality of the noble self from which they emanate. "It is obvious," says Friedrich Nietzsche in the latter work, "that moral designations were everywhere first applied to human beings and only after, derivatively, to actions." (Another way, quite different, of putting ethics in its place.) Walter Kaufmann (*From Shakespeare to Existentialism*) found the Nietzschean ideal in Shakespeare's Sonnet 94—"They that have the pow'r to hurt and will do none, / That do not do the things they most do show, / Who, moving others, are themselves as stone, / Unmoved, cold, and to temptation slow"—which Kaufmann compares to "Those who are sublime" in *Zarathustra*: "There is nobody from whom I want beauty as much as from you who are powerful; let your kindness be your final conquest. Of all evil I deem you capable; therefore I want the good from you. Verily, I have often laughed at the weaklings who thought themselves good because they had no claws."

Such a heady definition of a tested nobility of character:

the even cultivated capacity to do hurt but with the capacity restrained by the prerogatives of the noble self, not yielded to the defensive entreaties of society. But, it seems to me, it presupposes that the will to power can be contained by a kind of will to power over one's will to power—of which I don't feel too trusting. Furthermore, one cannot know whether or not he has a power-to-hurt to be restrained unless he has flexed that power—and the enterprise turns out to be essentially political, simply because the only place to discover and test the capacity is in the polis. So, there may be some distant comparison, but the sublime man of Nietzsche's imagining is not the Elect as I conceive of him or her. The Elect need have no political talents . . . or relevance.

Nor, for that very reason, has the Elect anything really to do with Jefferson's much more mildly imagined "natural aristocrat," who was, Jefferson wrote to John Adams, "the most precious gift of nature, for the instruction, the trusts, and the government of society. . . . May we not even say, that that form of government is best, which provides the most effectually for a pure selection of these natural aristoi into the office of government?" There is no rationally conceivable government that Emily Dickinson could or should officiate over.

So, the Elect. Not in the position of Calvin's grand elector, I can only risk a few impressions.

The Recluse of Amherst. Other recognized greats: Sophocles, Shakespeare, Goethe, Einstein—our tastes will differ, our judgments vary. Various evocative familiars, lesser but consequential, significant but not so certain: Randall Jarrell, William Hazlitt, mad Kit Smart, with whom Dr. Johnson would as leave pray as with any man, William James, the model for the *Job* poet if there was one, Mr. Bojangles.

Fictions and common realities: the girl with "neck curls, limp and damp as tendrils," for whom the poet Theodore Roethke mourned or the poet's father with "whiskey on your breath" that made "a small boy dizzy:" "You beat time on my head / With a palm caked hard by dirt, / Then waltzed me off to bed / Still clinging to your shirt."

One's private associations, unfamiliar to others: some relative with an unconscious talent for compassion, some friend with a talent for courage, turning affliction into an education of the soul. (As Flannery O'Connor wrote to Robert Fitzgerald: "I have never been anywhere but sick. In a sense sickness is a place, more instructive than a long trip to Europe, and it's always a place where there's no company, where nobody can follow.")

For most of us, life is not an adventure or sensed to be a gift, but is a mere state-that-is, as questioned as a fingernail. And for a few of us, life is a series of epiphanies. Most of us will not be a whit wiser, just more knowledgeable perhaps, when our terms here are over. And for a few, there will be some proportion between the luck to have lived and what they have perceived. The Elect.

There are only three ways the doctrine of Election and Damnation, as religious belief or secular metaphor, can be translated into politics. (1) You can long for an oligarchy of the Elect. But the search committee would have to be divinely wise, and would most certainly be swamped by confident applicants, the self-elected. (2) You can simply settle for an Elite. Or, (3) you can accept a sort of democracy of the Damned, and a few hidden Elect, and feel at least a little complimented that even so demanding a man as Jonathan Edwards knew that ordinary people, with their fractured motives and adoptive virtues, were responsible for the greater part of the moral action of the world.

WITTGENSTEIN AND THE
EMPEROR'S NEW CLOTHES

KENNETH FRANCIS

T HERE'S BEEN QUITE A LOT of intellectual praise written
about the over-rated philosopher Ludwig Wittgenstein
(1889-1951). The material is usually penned by academic disciples of Wittgenstein or by the dinner-party, dilettante, preten-
tious "intelligentsia" who like to drop his name to impart philosophical gravitas to their personas.

Now, I don't know what type of personality Wittgenstein
had, but I do know that most, not all, people who are hero-wor-
shiped by the shallow, chattering classes are degenerates or mo-
rons of the highest order. Also, the more obscure, vague and

ambiguous a celebrity intellectual is, the more the Great Woke Conformists will bestow virtue upon him or her.

There's nothing like a famous person talking from both sides of his mouth to win sycophant admirers. Speaking of which: I remember some 23 years ago, I attended a talk[1] by the late French philosopher, Jacques Derrida, who would've given Wittgenstein a run for his money regarding ambiguity.

What was remarkable about Derrida's lecture was he managed to deliver a convoluted and complicated talk to the delight of most of his audience. In words reminiscent of Gilbert and Sullivan's *Pirates of Penzance*,[2] he was "the very model of a major philosopher postmodernist."

Half-way through the lecture, I felt my head so phenomenologically deconstructed, I had to leave the building through the deafening applause of the circus-seals audience (maybe they were clapping at my departure!).

Anyhow, I later bumped into an excitable woman, in Waterstone's book store's philosophy section, who a week previously sat beside me during the Derrida lecture. With a massive grin and crazy eyes, she approached me saying, "Wasn't that a wonderful lecture?" I asked her what was the core message of the talk, as I was mystified. She looked at me blankly and smiled, "Sorry, I have to rush off now or I'll miss my bus." I've often thought that Derrida metaphorically "missed the bus." Or was it me who missed his point, during my then toxic blue-pilled days of brainwashed gullibility some 23 years ago?

As for those aboard the Wittgenstein bus: This essay will focus briefly on fringe aspects of Wittgenstein's biographical reputation and question his sources for knowledge in both the external world and in language.

I write "overrated" above because I believe any philosopher or writer who communicates in a chaotic way and confuses re-

---

1 Lecture by Jacques Derrida, entitled, "History Of The Lie, Lie Of The State," Theatre L, Arts Building, UCD college Dublin, Ireland, February 13, 1997.

2 I Am the Very Model of a Modern Major-General ("Modern Major-General's Song"), from Gilbert and Sullivan's 1879 comic opera *The Pirates of Penzance*.

ality engages in nothing short of a rejection of the Logos: Logic, Truth, Reason, God, Christ incarnate, Perfection, all things morally good. Outside of rational thought, it's easier to baffle people with B.S. than to dazzle them, like Christ did, with authentic brilliance.

As for Truth: The classic nineteenth-century story by Hans Christian Andersen, "The Emperor's New Clothes,"[3] reminds me of secular academia's high esteem for the ambiguous statements of Wittgenstein, particularly in his best-known and only *magnum opus, Tractatus Logico-Philosophicus.*[4]

In the Hans Christian Andersen tale, a couple of swindlers posing as weavers arrive in the city of an emperor who spends lots of money on clothes. They convince him that the suit they've woven for him is made of invisible thread, and they even mime dressing the emperor before he goes on a procession through the city.

But despite being naked, the emperor's officials and crowds in the city go along with the pretence for fear of looking stupid or having the "wrong" opinion (just like contemporary Woke conformists who gullibly believe anything the government or mainstream media tells them). Then a child shouts out that the emperor is wearing no clothes, and the people eventually realise they've been fooled.

The reason the Emperor's story reminds me of Wittgenstein is because I believe there's a possibility that most of his reputation relies on hype and myth. And when one is extremely wealthy, as Wittgenstein was, hype can open lots of doors and even manufacture dedicated disciples to worship you, especially if your message is a godless one in a world hostile to Christ; that's not to say Wittgenstein was anti-Christian.

For readers familiar with Wittgenstein's life, consider the following question: Is it possible for a billionaire to get someone to pretend for him that he was a front-line heroic soldier who fought in a world war? And that he inherited a fortune, gave it

---

3   Hans Christian Andersen, "The Emperor's New Clothes," published in *Fairy Tales Told for Children*, 1837.

4   Ludwig Wittgenstein, *The Tractatus Logico-Philosophicus*, (1921).

all away, designed aircraft and houses, and lived a chaste life? I'm not denying Wittgenstein didn't tick all those above boxes, but is there certainty (an alleged criterion Wittgenstein's philosophy hinges on) that he did such things?

For me, I cannot confirm nor deny the third-hand testimony of such statements on Wittgenstein's past prior to his fame at Trinity College, Cambridge; thereof, should I remain silent? Surely, I can speculate on his reputation, philosophy, and some biographical details that seem plausible?

For example, by way of analogy: Could a male actor "climbing the Hollywood ladder," who was an unknown young man in the 1970s, "sex-up" his resume to pretend he lived like a romantic drifter with an exotic past? And for an actor to lie on such biographical bull about his life during the internet/social-media-free seventies and eighties, he could claim he was a bullfighter in Italy, a private investigator in London, or a gigolo in Paris; how could it be proven he wasn't such exotic things? For all his fans know, in reality, he might've been a stable cleaner in Rome, a waiter in Paris, or a ticket man in Fulham Broadway Station.

In the Hollywood movie, *Being There,*[5] a simple-minded gardener is mistaken by politicians to be a genius. But his knowledge is based on the things he sees on TV. And though he rises to the top amongst the Washington elite, who see him as a great sage, the Secret Service is unable to find any information on his past/background.

But back to the wealthy bachelor Wittgenstein. With his piercing eyes and brooding guru looks, the enigmatic Austrian rose to fame far too quickly in Cambridge, under the wing of the godless, well-connected multimillionaire, Bertrand Russell.

Remember, regarding Wittgenstein's character, we're talking

---

5 *Being There*, directed by Hal Ashby, United Artists, 1979.

here about a suicidal,[6] alleged misogynist,[7] an inarticulate stutterer,[8] who once attacked a professor with a poker.[9] He also liked sitting in the front row of a cinema, while eating a cold pork pie, as he watched big macho cowboys on screen during the golden age of Westerns.[10] And let's not forget his time working as a teacher, when he bullied his pupils. Writing in *The Paris Review* (March 5, 2015), Spencer Robins said Wittgenstein's zeal also led him to abuse the children entrusted to him and added:

> It's hard now to know how consistent his use of corporal punishment was with standard practice at the time. He would strike students not just for misbehavior but for their failure to grasp the questions he put to them—and this led to the shameful end of his teaching career. One day, Wittgenstein hit a student named Haidbauer, who was sickly. When Haidbauer collapsed after the blow, Wittgenstein carried him to the headmaster's office and fled. A group of parents—who had apparently wanted Wittgenstein fired for some time—filed a complaint, which led to a hearing. He was cleared, ultimately, but he had already resigned, and years later he confessed to friends that he had lied at the hearing to protect himself. These events became known as the Haidbauer Incident, and they remained in the area's public memory for years.

6 "Letter to 'Mr 'E'" May 30, 1920. In these selections from the *Notebooks 1914–16* (which include a few entries, like the one presented here, from January 1917) and the letters of May 30 and June 21, 1920, to "Mr. E" (his friend Paul Engelmann, who subsequently edited the letters, as well as a letter of July 7, 1920, to Bertrand Russell), Wittgenstein discusses his confrontation with thoughts of suicide.

7 "Wittgenstein was very much against women's suffrage for no particular reason except that 'all women he knows are such idiots'." (Ray Monk, *Ludwig Wittgenstein: The Duty of Genius*).

8 *The New Book of Knowledge – Health and Medicine* (2001) pp. 112-123; Wiki reference for author, Richard Trubo.

9 *Wittgenstein's Poker: The Story of a Ten-Minute Argument Between Two Great Philosophers* is a 2001 book by BBC journalists David Edmonds and John Eidinow about events in the history of philosophy involving Sir Karl Popper and Ludwig Wittgenstein, leading to a confrontation at the Cambridge University Moral Sciences Club in 1946.

10 *Wittgenstein at the Movies: Cinematic Investigations*, edited by Bela Szabados and Christina Stojanova, Lexington Books, 2011 (p. 21).

Considering some of the above traits, did Russell commission a sleuth to do any background checks on his "genius" new friend Ludwig? I doubt it. Or did he just believe everything Wittgenstein told him because he liked what he heard, and his beliefs were based on his feelings? And what exactly was it that Russell heard from Wittgenstein?

The writer Crispin Sartwell said:

> When he first met Wittgenstein, Russell called him 'the most perfect example I have ever known of genius,' despite or perhaps because he couldn't understand what young Ludwig was saying. Writing to his lover Ottoline Morrell in 1913 about Wittgenstein's attack on one of his logical doctrines, Russell confessed: 'I couldn't understand his objection—in fact he was very inarticulate—but I felt in my bones that he must be right.' He added: 'I saw that I could not hope ever again to do fundamental work in philosophy.'
>
> That Wittgenstein's mysterious charisma disabled a philosopher and logician as brilliant as Russell was among the first of its baleful effects, and Russell did in fact largely abandon logic at that moment.[11]

Here are some core beliefs of Wittgenstein's philosophy: 1. The world is everything that is the case. 2. What is the case (a fact) is the existence of states of affairs. 3. A logical picture of facts is a thought. 4. A thought is a proposition with a sense. 5. A proposition is a truth-function of elementary propositions. 6. The general form of a proposition is the general form of a truth function. 7. Whereof one cannot speak, thereof one must be silent.

Ultimately, Wittgenstein's philosophy concludes in the *Tractatus Logico-Philosophicus* with: "My propositions serve as elucidations in the following way: anyone who understands me eventually recognizes them as nonsensical, when he has used them—as steps—to climb beyond them. (He must, so to speak,

---

11   Crispin Sartwell, "Overrated: Ludwig Wittgenstein," *Standpoint*, September 18, 2019.

throw away the ladder after he has climbed up it.)" In other words, he must transcend these propositions, and then he will see the world aright.

Sartwell maintained that Russell turned Wittgenstein into an intellectual superstar: "Ever since, Wittgenstein has been more of a cult than an argument, an irrationalist movement in a supposedly rational discipline. Like Russell, Wittgenstein's followers know he is right; the only difficulty is knowing what he meant."

Even the famous photo of him standing in front of a wall that resembles a Jackson Pollock "action painting," aptly depicts the chaos going through this tortured Austrian's head. But not every intellectual who knew of Wittgenstein fell under his spell.

Anthony Quinton, later Lord Quinton, in his *From Wodehouse to Wittgenstein*,[12] questions the assertion that Wittgenstein is the greatest twentieth-century philosopher, but admits that "he remains the object of a fair-sized and energetically devotional cult, a continuation of the circle of profoundly self-abasing disciples with which he surrounded himself from his return from Austria to Cambridge in 1929 until the end of his life."

The author/researcher Ibn Warraq says he remembers attending classes at the University of London in the 1970s on Wittgenstein's *Tractatus Logico-Philosophicus*, given by Hide Ishiguro, who later went on to teach at Columbia University. Warraq said: "I can only describe her lectures as 'religious sermons', with the *Tractatus* as the Holy Text. The reverence for each obscure or banal statement was profound, and one did not contradict or interrupt the religious ecstasy. We were warned against taking seemingly simple sentences at face value: they all hid profound insights, and truths that no other human being had hitherto glimpsed."[13]

I would never want Wittgenstein's work cancelled, as I think

---

12   Anthony Quinton, *From Wodehouse to Wittgenstein*, Carcanet Press, Manchester (UK), 1998 (p. 335).
13   Comment in *New English Review* on an essay by Samuel Hux, entitled "Demoting Wittgenstein, Mourning Trumbull Stickney" (See page 27.)

the value of a thinker's philosophical ideas have no bearing on any defects of his or her personal character. However, I take Wittgenstein's legacy seriously, because I think his philosophy has the potential to be influential and dangerous, especially in a world where the dominant message is "perception is reality" and "truth is relative." Jesus was all about Truth. And had he a message for Wittgenstein, I'm confident it would be Matthew 5:37: "But let your communication be, Yea, yea; Nay, nay: for whatsoever is more than these cometh of evil."[14]

---

14 *The Bible*, Matthew 5:37, King James version.

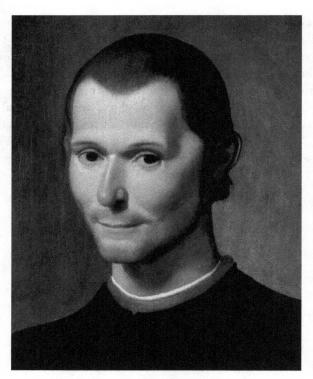

NICCOLÒ MACHIAVELLI

THEODORE DALRYMPLE

WHETHER NICCOLÒ MACHIAVELLI WAS a philosopher in the strict sense depends on one's definition of philosophy. Certainly, he was a lover of wisdom, if only of a narrow kind: that necessary to a ruler who wants to maintain himself in power. His work nevertheless raises questions of political philosophy that to this day have not been definitively answered.

He has long had a very bad reputation, of course, as being of the party of the Devil. The adjective Machiavellian denotes ruthlessness in pursuit of an ambition, and a willingness to lie,

intrigue, deceive and betray in order to gain one's ends. As to
the moral quality of the ends themselves to be achieved by these
methods, Machiavelli does not say a great deal. It is evident that
he is against violent anarchism, regarding almost anything as
better than that, which is not surprising considering the time
and place in which he lived—one of constant warring between
the petty states in Italy which permitted foreign intervention
and domination—but he has no elevated ethical end of political
action in view. He is a radical realist, often seeming to regard
power as a good in itself, like a Renaissance Nietszche.

Christopher Marlowe, in his play *The Jew of Malta*, makes
Machiavelli (under the name of Machiavel) speak the prologue,
in which he says:

> I count religion but as a childish toy,
> And hold there is no sin but ignorance.
> Birds of the air will tell of murders past?
> I am ashamed to hear such fooleries.

He is unconcerned by the opprobrium in which he is held:

> Admired I am of those that hate me most.
> Though some speak openly against my books,
> Yet they will read me...

Marlowe himself was suspected of atheism and of being a Machiavellian; and he was right, Machiavelli has been read ever
since. And certainly, there are passages in *The Prince*, the short
book that has immortalised Machiavelli, that suggest that Machiavelli's attitude to religion was one of ironic detachment,
rather like Gibbon's a quarter of a millennium later. Speaking of
those great leaders who have achieved power by their own great
talent and exertions, Machiavelli says:

> I say that the most outstanding are Moses, Cyrus, Romulus,
> Theseus, and others like them. Although one should not rea-
> son about Moses, since he merely executed what God com-
> manded, yet he must be praised for the grace which made him

worthy of speaking with God. But let us consider Cyrus and
the others who acquired and founded kingdoms: they were
all praiseworthy, and their actions and institutions, when ex-
amined, do not seem to differ from those of Moses, who has
such a mighty teacher. And when we come to examine their
lives, they do not seem to have had from fortune anything
other than opportunity.

In other words, God's teaching was an unnecessary hypothesis
in the case of Moses. Or again, discussing the power of ecclesiastical states, he says:

> They are maintained, in fact, by religious institutions, so pow-
> erfully mature that, no matter how the ruler acts and lives,
> they safeguard his government... But as they are sustained by
> higher powers which the human mind cannot comprehend, I
> shall not argue about them; they are exalted and maintained
> by God, and so only a rash and presumptuous man would
> take it on himself to discuss them. Nonetheless, if anyone
> should ask me how it is that the Church has attained such
> great temporal power, inasmuch as, up to the time of Alex-
> ander [VI], the Italian potentates, and not only those who are
> called potentates but every baron and nobleman, even the
> pettiest, set it at naught, but now a king of France trembles
> before it, and it has been able to chase him out of Italy and
> ruin the Venetians, I should not think it superfluous to recall
> to some extent how it happened, even though the story is well
> known.

Compare this with Gibbon's introduction, in his *Decline and
Fall of the Roman Empire*, of his explanation of how Christianity
became the dominant religion of Europe:

> Our curiosity is naturally prompted to inquire by what means
> the Christian faith obtained so remarkable a victory over the
> established religions of the earth. To this inquiry an obvious
> but unsatisfactory answer may be returned: that it was own-
> ing to the convincing evidence of the doctrine itself, and to
> the ruling providence of its great Author. But as truth and
> reason seldom find so favourable a reception in the world,

and as the wisdom of Providence frequently condescends to use the passions of the human heart, and the general circumstances of mankind, as instruments to execute its purpose, we may still be permitted, though with becoming submission, to ask, not indeed what were the first, but what were the secondary causes of the rapid growth of the Christian church?

The parallels between Machiavelli's and Gibbon's thought are clear. Both are committed to naturalistic explanations of historical events: they are realists rather than idealists. "I have thought it better," says Machiavelli in *The Prince*, "to represent things as they are in a real truth, rather than as they are imagined." He is resolutely anti-utopian and against the kind of thought which dreams up the blueprint of a perfect state of affairs and would then encourage or force men to pursue such a chimera. "Many have dreamed up republics and principalities which have never in truth been known to exist; the gulf between how one should live and how one does live is so wide that a man who neglects what is actually done for what should be done moves towards self-destruction rather than self-preservation."

A realist of Machiavelli's type needs what might be called a philosophical anthropology, or doctrine of human nature. The problem with such a doctrine is that it is likely to derive from the author's experience, which is of necessity limited both in time and place. This would not matter if human nature were the same in all times and in all places, but that is precisely the question at issue. And no one can know all times and all places.

Machiavelli assumes, for example, that men strive for domination over their fellows or have a tendency to do so. Of course, he does not claim that all men without exception so strive; the claim is only that there will always be, in any likely society, a number of men who do, and that is sufficient for his purposes. It will create the struggle for power, and the struggle to retain it, which is his subject.

But is he right? Are there always men who seek to dominate, or is it conceivable that one day, under some different dispensation from any that we know, domination of his fellows will attract no man?

I do not know much of the anthropological literature that describes very different societies from our own and that might provide a positive, though not a negative, answer to this question. Somewhere there might have been a society of some complexity and sophistication in which there was no competition for power, status, wealth, etc. But if there were a description of such a society, I should be reluctant to believe it, on the grounds that led Hume to reject the possibility of miracles: that the likelihood of the thing reported was less than the likelihood that the report was erroneous.[1]

Be that as it may, I think that for all practical purposes Machiavelli was correct in his assumption: that in any society of size and complexity, there will always be at least some men who wish to dominate. This gives rise to the question as to how

---

1   Anthropologists, like everyone else, are prone to error. A case in point was brought to light by the Australian anthropologist, Derek Freeman, in his book: *The Fateful Hoaxing of Margaret Mead*. According to Freeman, Mead's informants on the islands of Samoa deliberately misled her about their sexual practices during adolescence and told her what she evidently wanted to hear, laughing behind her back at her gullibility. This was not without significance for the Western world, for a few decades after the publication of her book, *Coming of Age in Samoa*, it was used as evidence that there could exist a sexuality free of all the inhibitions that gave rise to the guilt and anxiety associated with sex in the West. It was used as an instrument in the sexual revolution, according to which sex could be liberated from constraint without any concomitant drawbacks. If Freeman was right, this was based on mistaken or false anthropological evidence; and certainly the sexual revolution has thrown up problems of its own.

Another example is that of Colin Turnbull's book, *The Mountain People*, in which an African tribe, the Ik, are described who were utterly without concern for one another, not even for their own children or parents, and who rejoiced or laughed at the misfortunes of their fellows such as serious injury and illness. This was deemed significant, because it suggested that Man has no natural propensity to good, and that, for example, Adam Smith's assertion at the beginning of his book, *The Theory of Moral Sentiments*, is simply false: "How selfish soever man may be supposed to be, there are evidently some principles in his nature, which interest him in the fortune of others, and render their happiness necessary to him, though he derives nothing from it except the pleasure of seeing it." The description of a thousand societies of which this is the case does not prove it to be true; the description of one society of which this is not the case proves it to be false.

power is to be achieved, distributed, controlled and maintained, with the risk that the struggle for power will become so acute that it destroys or enfeebles the society in which it takes place.

Machiavelli, in his advice to the "prince" who is establishing his power, who in our time is likely to be a democratically-elected politician, makes psychological observations which may or may not be true for all times and places—he does not consider the question, but since many of his examples of how people behave are taken from remote antiquity, we may assume that he believes in stable human propensities.

His view of humanity is not altogether flattering. In the mass, Man is for him inconstant, fickle, untrustworthy, just as he was for Shakespeare; it is easy to persuade the populace of something, he says, but difficult to fix it in their minds. He says that one can generalise about men, and that they are ungrateful, fickle, liars, and deceivers, that they shun danger and are eager for profit. Machiavelli wrote at a time when people did not think to provide evidence for their generalisations by means of statistics, but one can at least say that one knows what he means.

Men in general, he says, judge by superficial appearances, so that the "prince" should appear to the people to be a man of compassion, good faith, integrity and religion, with the implication that he should be none of these things. (One thinks of Richard, in *Richard III*, who—preposterously—poses as a devout man between two clerics in order to win the approbation of the London mob.)

Machiavelli says that men forgive the unjust death of their fathers at the hand of the prince more easily than they forgive the despoliation of their property by him. For this to be even partially true, there must first be property, of course: it couldn't be true of a propertyless society. And if this disturbing dictum seems to be too harsh a judgment of the whole of mankind, yet common experience demonstrates that there is an element of truth in it, for it is undoubtedly the case that to this day some members of families place a higher value on the preservation of material wealth than on the life of their own parents. Machiavelli exaggerates, but for something to be an exaggeration, it must contain a grain of truth.

Again, Machiavelli tells us that a man may be hated as much for his good deeds as for his bad, especially in a population in which vice is widespread. There is a Hindi saying pointing to the same truth: *Why do you hate me, for I have never tried to do anything for you?* Virtue is a reproach to vice, just as beauty is to ugliness: and men are not fond of reproaches. Thus, if they can achieve neither, they may come to hate both; and since both vice and ugliness are easier of attainment than their opposites, the prevalence of the former may grow until they become predominant. This is especially so in a society that specifically rejects any aristocratic sensibility.

When a man has a bad conscience, Machiavelli says in his *Discourses*, he readily believes that people are talking about him, and an innocent remark takes on a significance that it does not really have: he has what modern-day psychiatrists call ideas of reference.

Machiavelli also notes the relative fixity of men's characters, and the problems this may bring with it. Different circumstances call for different qualities, at least in that they are to be negotiated with success. Cesare Borgia, a man of triumphant success while his father, Pope Alexander VI lived, did not realise that the subsequent Pope, Julius II, an inveterate enemy of the previous incumbent, would never be other than his enemy and could never be inveigled into alliance with him, and therefore continuation on his old path had become impossible. He assumed that the methods that had brought him success in the past would continue to do so; he did not realise that "whoever believes that with great men new services wipe out old injuries deceives himself." Machiavelli says the same of Julius II: that had he not died at the height of his success, he too would have failed in the end, because the times were changing and he would have proved too rigid to change with them. Success, according to Machiavelli, is brought about by a convergence of circumstance and character, and character is not easily changed.

Psychological observations of this kind are important, because the "prince" has to deal with realities: he must know how people are rather than how he would like them to be. And in his *The Way to Treat the People of the Valley of China in Revolt,* he says:

> The world has always been inhabited by men with the same passions; there have always been people who served and people who commanded; people who served reluctantly and others willingly; people who rebelled and people who were punished.

This has important implications. If passions are the same always and everywhere, it is useless to expect fundamental change in mankind. If they were not the same, there would be little point in studying history, apart from the pleasure of satisfying idle curiosity, for it would have nothing useful to teach us. Even the Marxist scheme of history assumes that people in like circumstances will behave in the same way.

Does this mean that Machiavelli is, in his prescriptions, either totally immoral or amoral? Does might for him make right?

If we examine his arguments in the *Discourses* against the construction and maintenance of fortresses in towns and cities, for example, we can deduce that he is not devoid of normal moral sense. There are two possible uses of fortresses in a town or city, says Machiavelli: first, to protect it against external enemies who besiege it, the second to protect its rulers from the wrath of the population. In either case, the fortress will prove useless: external enemies will have sufficient artillery to batter down its walls, and if the rulers have to take refuge in it against their own populations, all is lost for them in any case. The reason for having to take such refuge can only be that they, the rulers, have stirred the population to revolt by their oppression and depredations, and no one could possibly think that Machiavelli uses such words as terms of approbation. True, he does not describe what he means by oppression, perhaps because for him it is so obvious that further elaboration is unnecessary. What needs not be said needs not be said. But it is obvious that Machiavelli has a conception of the public good, which he believes should be promoted or at least not harmed: for he believes that what most people desire of their government is that it should leave them alone while securing public order.

Machiavelli makes an implicit distinction between public and private morality. They overlap but are not identical. What is good in private may not be good in public life. While cruelty, for example, is always a vice in private life, it may be necessary in public:

> I believe that here it is a question of cruelty used well or badly. We can say that cruelty is used well (if it is permissible to talk in this way of what is evil) when it is employed once and for all, and one's safety depends on it, and then it is not persisted in, but as far as possible turned to the good of one's subjects. Cruelty badly used is that which, although infrequent to start with, as time goes on, rather than disappearing, grows in intensity.

Here Machiavelli hints at the fact of human psychology, that appetite grows with the feeding and escapes its original scope, notoriously so in the case of cruelty, whose exercise becomes a pleasure and a necessity in itself. More importantly, he suggests that the exercise of cruelty is sometimes necessary in political life. "By making an example or two," he says, "he will prove more compassionate that those who, being too compassionate, allow disorders which lead to murder and rapine. These nearly always harm the whole community, whereas executions ordered by the prince only affect individuals."

Political life imposes moral imperatives different from those of private life, and one cannot simply transfer private virtues to public life, only on a larger scale (a misapprehension that is commonplace today, when governments feel compelled to demonstrate their compassion and leaders claim to feel everyone's pain). "The fact is," says Machiavelli, "that a man who wants to act virtuously in every way necessarily comes to grief among so many who are not virtuous."

The ability to dissemble is valuable for a "prince," because it is useful for him to have a reputation for virtue while performing acts usually considered to be vicious. Nevertheless, he must not let a desire for such a reputation stand in his way when ruthlessness is required:

> This is because, taking everything into account, he will find that some of the things that appear virtues will, if he practices them, ruin him, and some of the things that appear to be vices will bring him security and prosperity.

The difference between public and private morality is evident in everyday life. Should one give money to beggars in the street, especially in countries with social security systems that prevent absolute destitution? One does not want to encourage mendicancy, of course, which generosity can only encourage. On the other hand, beggary is not a happy condition, however much reduction to it may be the fault of the beggar himself, and a small donation will lift the spirits of the beggar, if only momentarily, and to lift human spirits at little cost to oneself is surely a laudable thing to do. Stories of beggars who make a good living from their activity and return from the street to live in luxury are surely apocryphal, an excuse to justify lack of generosity, and even if a case could be found in which it were true— well, it would be an exception, and as Doctor Johnson said, it is better sometimes to be deceived than never to trust. But the desirable aim of eliminating beggary will never be achieved by the aggregate effect of thousands of small acts of generosity, a personal virtue, and might even make it more prevalent. If begging never worked, there would be no beggars (and in current circumstances, those who might have been beggars otherwise would not starve as a result). Private sentiments cannot be the basis of public policy; personal morality is different from political economy.

The problem of the relationship of politics to morality, so present in Machiavelli, is still with us: the two poles being those of idealism on the one hand and realism on the other. Machiavelli is usually taken to be at the realist end of the spectrum, but I think he is somewhere towards the middle. He is, after all, an Italian nationalist, as well as a local Florentine patriot, who deeply resents humiliating foreign interference in the affairs of the Italian peninsula, and who is appalled at the military weakness that has enabled and encouraged this. Italian military efforts are directed at internecine quarrels between Italian city states over small tracts of land, and even here are vitiated by the frequent employment of mercenary troops which are unreliable, cowardly, and rapacious. They run away when seriously threatened; they are more interested in loot than in fighting; they are often rebellious because they go unpaid; having no local or national loyalty, they are not prepared to die, for they have no cause to die for. A soldier who is not prepared to die in battle is unlikely to fight ardently. Machiavelli makes the interesting opposite point, only too relevant in these times of fanatical terrorism: "Princes cannot escape death if the attempt is made by a fanatic, because anyone who has no fear of death himself can succeed in inflicting it." It is not only princes, alas, who have to fear fanatics.

For Machiavelli, the invading foreigners are "barbarians." By this, he cannot mean that they behave barbarically, as we should now think it, for he describes on several occasions actions by the Italians themselves that we should call barbaric. What he must mean, then, is that the foreigners are barbarians because they are deficient in the arts of civilisation, not because they loot, pillage and decapitate—which the Italians themselves do when "necessary." In this matter, Machiavelli's sensibility is very different from the contemporary one: for no matter how flourishing the arts of a country may be, we should not call it civilised if it changed leaders by means of poison, decapitation, and throat-cutting, often during or in the wake of banquets, as was often the case in Machiavelli's Italy. Winston Churchill himself once said that the state of a country's civilisation may be judged by how it treated its prisoners, in which case Renaissance Italy could hardly be called civilised. (When he fell from grace in Florence after the restoration of the Medici, Machiavelli was tortured during his imprisonment.) But it seems to me that Churchill was foreshadowing the sentimentality of our times in his remark, a sentimentality that is in its own way uncivilised, for it makes a single desideratum—the decent treatment of prisoners—the sole criterion of civilisation itself, which then excuses or even encourages barbarism in other directions such as art and architecture: and who comparing the city of Coventry, say, with Ferrara, would come to the conclusion that ours is a civilisation in all respects on a higher plane than that of Renaissance Italy? If we took seriously what Churchill said (albeit that it was meant humanely), we should have to say that civilisation began with Elizabeth Fry, the prison reformer, and then only very tentatively.

Machiavelli's desire to rid the Italian peninsula of foreign invaders is an ideal, but clearly not a universal one, since it concerns only Italy. It is a practical ideal, whose aim is to remove a harm rather than to promote a good, at least a good in the sense of an ideal society, which Machiavelli never suggests that the removal of the foreigners would produce. "In politics," he said, "the choice is rarely between good and evil, but between the worst and the less bad." But the very idea of the worst and the less bad necessarily implies a scale of values.

Machiavelli clearly believes that the end justifies the means, at least in politics. He is a consequentialist in ethics, rather than a deontologist. Circumstances alter cases; invariable rules cannot be given, because the application of the same rule will produce a very different result in one circumstance from another, good in the first and disastrous in the second. Moreover, circumstances are infinitely variable.

In politics, the difference in the two kinds of ethics is between idealism and realism. This is a dilemma that is still with us. Should a county's foreign policy, for example, be the pursuit of an ideal, or should it simply be the pursuit of a national interest? There are clearly drawbacks to both. Machiavelli obviously is on the side of realism, but as we have seen, that does not exclude all moral considerations.

A man who has no principles is a scoundrel; a man who has only principles is a fool or a fanatic. Whether scoundrels or fools and fanatics do more harm in the world is a matter that is perhaps not susceptible of definitive answer. The proper approach to politics, one can deduce from Machiavelli, is a balance between principle and realistic possibility.

The achievement of such a balance is very difficult. One cannot be morally required to do what is impossible for one to do; one cannot be responsible for what one is powerless to effect or change. But the estimation of the degree of one's power or powerlessness is not straightforward; it depends not only on tangible factors, such as military strength, but intangible ones such as willingness to make sacrifices. Even military strength is not easy to estimate. An army can be huge and well-equipped, but if it has low morale, if it refuses to fight, if it does not believe in what it is doing, it will be nugatory. Machiavelli, for whom history was a kind of laboratory from which to draw lessons, would, if he were alive today, illustrate this point by reference to the defeat of Batista's army in Cuba, Mobutu's in Zaire, the Shah's in Iran, the government's in Afghanistan, among others. Moreover, the state of the enemy's army cannot be known for sure. Its capacity may be under- or overestimated. The Japanese were underestimated successively by the Russians, the British and the Americans. The Egyptians underestimated the Israelis, and then, in 1973, the Israelis returned the compliment. One easily believes what one wants to believe rather than what the evidence should lead one to believe. Rationalisation is easier than rationality. Reasons both for action and inaction can easily be found. The wish is not only father to the thought but to the selection of evidence in favour of that thought.

The person who is guided wholly or mainly by his ideals risks becoming a Don Quixote. He is inclined to disregard the possibility of unintended consequences to his well-intended actions; he sees a people or country in distress, the consequence of foreign oppression, say, and rushes to its aid. Alas, he is soon mired in unlooked-for complications. The oppressed turn out to be as bad as the oppressors; their leaders are not struggling for freedom but for power and the opportunity to oppress in their turn. What seems at first an easy task proves to be very difficult. The assumption that the liberated population is thirsting for democracy turns out to be false; they have no idea what democracy means, other than liberty for themselves.

On the other hand, making pacts with the devil is also hazardous. People are revolted by it, and the state of public opinion is itself a force to be reckoned with. Moreover, the devil cannot be trusted to keep his word; he devours those who befriend him. But foreign affairs can no more be decided by private morality than can political economy. In private life, one can often (not always) avoid distasteful people; but dealings with hostile or repugnant governments are necessary and sometimes essential. They may, for example, have control of what you need; it may in certain circumstances be necessary to ally yourself with them, if there is a worse enemy to be confronted.

Politics is never Newtonian physics; it is action in multiple fields of ignorance with occasional patches of knowledge. Thus, all political principles have exceptions and no outcome is assured. The unpredictable and unexpected often upsets the best calculations. What is wise in one circumstance is foolish in another.

Machiavelli is often taken as an apostle of evil: so great a thinker as Raymond Aron took him as such. Bertrand Russell thought *The Prince* a manual for gangsters. But I do not think this is right. Doing what is good requires no defenders, but Machiavelli was concerned to show that what was right in politics is not just a projection on a larger screen of private morality; rather, politics often entailed actions that would be reprehensible in private life, but he did not, therefore, grant *carte blanche* to political actors.

From a modern perspective, he often reads as a cynic—but a highly intelligent one to whom any aspiring politician would do well to attend. He tells us that the "prince" should do everything possible to make the population dependent on him, which is precisely the policy of so many governments half a millennium later; and he tells us that the "prince" should delegate to others those measures which are likely to prove unpleasant and unpopular, to divert attention from his own responsibility for them. This, surely, is sound advice. But a cynic is a disappointed moralist, not a person of no moral outlook whatever.

Machiavelli is ambiguous, because life is ambiguous and

cannot be made otherwise. Even the two accounts of his death suggest ambiguity. On one account, he confessed on his death-bed and underwent the last rites of the Catholic Church. On the other account, he had a dream in which he saw two groups of people, the first miserably dressed and the second well-dressed, whom he recognised as the great thinkers of the past. He asked the two groups who they were. The first replied that they were the blessed and were going to heaven. The second said that they were the damned and were going to hell, because knowledge of this world was the enemy of God.

Waking from his dream, Machiavelli said, "I would prefer to go to hell to discuss politics with them than go to heaven with imbeciles."

Which of these stories of his end is true? One, both, or nei-ther?

PLATO, RELEVANT STILL:
THE CONCEPT OF THE UNIQUELY
APPROPRIATE

SAMUEL HUX

BACK WHEN I WAS A SOCIALIST, a card-carrying member first of DSOC (Democratic Socialist Organizing Committee), and then its successor DSA (Democratic Socialists of America), and a regular contributor to *Dissent* . . . I was aware, fully so, of the darker possibilities inherent in the socialist vision. After all, one would have to be stupid not to know that what was often called (in contradistinction to ideologues' dreams of what might be) "actually existing socialism" (that is, communism), was not merely a passing Stalinist aberration. One reason for the awareness was the observable mentality of some of one's colleagues (but not the best of them, my old friend and mentor Irving Howe for instance), the arrogant and almost limitless certainty and impatience with nuance, that which is so observable today in the unearned confidence brooking no dissent of the Bernie Sanders era Left.

The ellipsis in the preceding paragraph just before "I was aware" should indicate an interruption. Because I was about to say, "Back when I was a socialist, I was even then a conservative." I remember briefly calling myself a "Left Conservative." (I think it was Norman Mailer who invented the term, to distinguish himself from the young "New Leftists:" "I'm not sure I want a revolution. Some of these kids are awfully dumb.") That is, I thought democratic socialism would be more respectful of and conserving of what was best in Western civilization, in Judeo-Christendom if you will, in the "permanent things" as Russell Kirk used to say. Well, I have made my peace with democratic socialism's rival, capitalism—but it is a peace which has not dispensed with alert border guards. For now that I am a conservative without "left-" as an adjectival prefix, I am aware, fully so, of the darker possibilities inherent in the capitalist vision. I don't delude myself that I am alone among conservatives in this respect: I am fond of quoting that Hungarian-American Tory, John Lukacs, that conservatives cannot be capitalist enthusiasts. But this is not precisely the focus of this essay. Rather:

On the American scene at least—which is where I am looking—there are several varieties of self-proclaimed conservatives. Not to make an uncontrollable list, there are "The Traditionalists" (I hold up my hand and announce, "Present!"); there are "The Paleo-Conservatives" (*Paleo-Cons*), who have such contempt for "The Neo-Conservatives" (*Neo-Cons*); and there may be a slew of single-issue brands as well, not only "The Libertarians" about whom more later.

But there is one brand which has no identifying name (as yet), although it is very large in enrollment I am sure. Every single subscriber to this brand I have ever met personally is a male, so I can dispense with the *he-or-she* and *him-or-her* verbal badge of political correctness. The virtues and values that have traditionally marked a conservative disposition have little purchase for him. He is not concerned with religious values, the cultural heritage, the sanctity of traditional marriage, you-name-it; questions of the size of government are no big deal, except in so far as politics impinges on economic issues. His one big thing is the worship of and defense of capitalism. That is the extent of his "conservatism." Privately I think of him as a "Putative Conservative," or if you will (or even if you won't), a *Put-Con*.

Since I don't think the Put-Con necessarily understands the economic faith which he worships, what follows is a discussion of that faith and his relationship to it.

As a function (forget *ideologies* for the moment) of what we blithely call "capitalism" is an arrangement whereby capital formed by any of several means (money being a human convenience, not a creation of nature) is put to work in production of goods manufactured by labor, which is paid neither the unknowable intrinsic value of its time nor the impossible-to-ascertain "true" worth of its energy for the creation of capital surpluses. But what is done with those surpluses, beyond sufficient reinvestment in the process, is a question not of fictive metaphysical laws of production or appeals to inexorable Economic Nature, but of ethics. And distribution of surpluses is one matter "capitalist ethics" are loath to reflect upon. For reflection might reveal, if done in public, the capitalist's historical and conventional *but not necessary* relevance to the capitalist *function*. The function does not require the traditional capitalist: it requires somebody or some Body to form a sufficient accumulation of that human convenience. And any economy, beyond primitive bartering, requires the function. Nor are *markets* uniquely characteristic of capitalism. They are characteristic of a sophisticated economy; and it is only the Put-Con's prejudice that renders the meaning of "markets" and "capitalism" as being the same. As the shrewd Scottish economist Alec Nove once observed, even in a centrally planned command economy you can't do without markets; for while a planning board can predict with fair accuracy how many pairs of shoes will be needed, only a market can tell you which sizes.

But, as one seldom asks in public a question he thinks he has no answer to (that's the trial lawyer in all of us), I would like to suggest an answer to my own question: What is this capitalism? The word itself is inherently ambiguous, referring both to a direction of socio-economic arrangements and to a public philosophy in defense of that direction. I'm going to argue that what most deeply characterizes the direction (as the capital function and markets do not) and most deeply characterizes the priorities in the public philosophy is the rejection of what I will call "the concept of the *uniquely appropriate*."

And, as one sometimes does ask in public a question he'd like an answer to but suspects he doesn't have it yet (that's the law student in all of us), I would like to wonder aloud why conservatives, who traditionally are supposed to be enamored of words like "the appropriate," "propriety," and so on, would by and large embrace so enthusiastically a system (as Put-Cons certainly do) and would contribute so energetically to an ideology both of which reject such notions.

When I began this line of thought, I was not aware how Platonic my reasoning was. I surely should have been aware, because I have been talking to students about Plato for no short time, especially *The Republic*. And while I tell my students that I think utopian political thinking has borne ill fruit in actual political history, and I would not wish to live in Plato's Kallipolis, his ideal city, any more than I would wish to live in any of the totalitarian experiments that have seen the actual light of historical day, I nonetheless find something worthy in his idea of what makes his tripartite state just. Quick lesson or reminder, as the case may be:

Socrates makes a basic analogy between individual soul and collective *polis* (although his process of moving from state to soul is the reverse of my following process). Just as the just soul has three parts—the Appetitive, the *Thumos* (often translated as "spiritedness" or "courage"), and the Rational—with the three parts doing what they should do and not something else, as Reason rather than the Appetites governs the person and as Thumos protects and aggresses when necessary, the state is equally tripartite: Artisans or Producers (farmers, carpenters, weavers, etc.) seeing to the fulfillment of basic appetitive needs for food, shelter, clothing, and such; Guards seeing to the soldierly protection of the population; and Rulers seeing to the rational governance of all. And the polis is just in so far as Producers produce and do not try to play soldier-boy, and Rulers rule and do not try to farm or weave or build houses, and so on, and Guards stick to their military tasks. This, thus, the ideal Republic.

Now, given the Platonic fact that if you are born to a farmer, there's a 99 percent chance that will be your lot in life—no yuppies encouraged—it is hard for us to imagine Plato and Socrates have discovered the key to happiness, but Socrates insists that all citizens, no matter which class, will indeed be happy because each will be doing what he or she is uniquely suited to do, as, for instance, soldiers will be happy to realize their native selves in selfless risk and would be bored stiff doing farm chores instead, etcetera, and so forth, *und so weiter.* Still I confess, as I confess to my students (no point in them thinking their professor a damned fool) that I would feel terribly uncomfortable in a state where the rulers commanded, "You will do what you are best suited to do. . . so go do it!" And, it is not only the being told what is best for me to do that I would find offensive, but more than that the over-confidence and extreme rationality behind the commands: extreme rationalists who want a perfectly ordered world seem to me to have insufficient appreciation (or none) for tradition, which tends to be a mixture of the orderly and the muddled. But be that as it will be, after my confession I have to admit that—the fate of any individual aside—it seems a very good idea that Producers, Soldiers, and Governors know what their job is and do not confuse the nature of one part of the tripartite with another. Producers are, let us say, *private citizens*—while Soldiers and Governors are, let us call them, *public servants.* You don't want in Plato's *polis* the military and the political leaders saying they think they will privatize their duties and see what their talents are worth in cash on the market; you

don't want Farmers and Carpenters and Clothiers trying to na-
tionalize their naturally private industries as it were.

Just as justice reigns in the individual soul when the three
parts/aspects are doing what they should be doing, and injustice reigns when, for dramatic instance, the individual is mis-
governed by a rampant appetite for satisfaction of the give-me
urge—so in the state justice reigns when the tripartite structure
is not fragmented by ignorance of or intentional defiance of "the
concept of the uniquely appropriate."

Due reverence to Plato—but now back to "the Now."

Some ideas have more traction than others, and those
that do seem to me to have two characteristics. (1) They have
a grip on us by virtue of being related, however indirectly, to
our livelihoods; there's nothing reticent about their action. (2)
While strong, "gripping," they are not advertised as ideas; they
become muted assumptions you simply do not have to think
much about, as if to say, "What other assumptions could a sane
person have?"

For example, in a fully capitalist society, the responsibility
for capital formation is assumed primarily by the capitalist in
such a way that although the capital invested may not be all his
creation, it is treated as if it were indeed all his creation—so
much so that the surplus that arises through the process of production is thought (to give a nice name to a mere mental reflex)
to be primarily *his* to reinvest if, where, and how *he* pleases,
and is thought to be *his* to distribute no more than *he* pleases.
Or, since facts of life such as labor unions impinge, when he is
forced to distribute more than he pleases, he is thought to be
distributing nonetheless that which is really *his*. In other words,
neither he nor the society at large will consider the part of the
surplus that is his to be really part of the surplus. An idea as
muted assumption is reigning.

But this is to speak of the quality of an idea, and the instance
I give need not be unique to a capitalist society. For with a
change of cast, the state replacing the private capitalist, that part
of the surplus which becomes the state's would not be thought
to be part of the surplus. So I probe further for the specific idea

which characterizes capitalism.

A traditional view of the "public sector" is that it performs tasks that are appropriate to it, but not appropriate to the "private sector:" whether nationalization in a mixed economy, or whether exercises we simply do not normally think of as nationalization, such as the military, infrastructure, or penal institutions. In a loose formation: the state handles what the state should handle because it should. But Robert Heilbroner made a brilliant observation (chapter 4 of *The Nature and Logic of Capitalism*) which I would like to consider in a way for which I'll not hold him responsible: Actually, under capitalism, the state *relieves* the private sector of functions which are *necessary* to the private sector but which would not be judged *profitable* to the private sector.

The state, that is, takes the heat off institutions of the private sector by disburdening them of responsibility for tasks they couldn't make money from, although the fulfillment of the tasks may be necessary even for the functioning of the private institution. This is not innocent. It is not an instance of the state performing certain tasks which ensure the quality of life for us all—as when, for mundane example, the township fills in the potholes on that road near the mineral spring which is closed for being polluted. Rather, the state performs X function because for perfectly graspable reasons no private corporation wants to. So, not a matter of *propriety* at all. As a corollary, it seems to me, if the private sector sees a potential profit in a task heretofore deemed appropriate to the public sector, it will, with state acquiescence or encouragement, move in. (Which is why the parenthetical question mark after "penal institutions" some paragraphs back.) And the part of the private sector that moves in is most likely not going to be some small, minimally capitalized proprietorship (Al and Eileen's Ltd.), but more likely some heavy which is sufficient to the task of replacing the government. So no Put-Con or any other capitalist apologist need talk here about the distribution of opportunity, need sing no small-is-beautiful songs in celebration of the brave entrepreneur.

Some would protest that the state does not *yield the profitable* to the private sector, but rather *relieves itself* of the burden (perhaps responding to enthusiasts for "privatization" who like to pretend they're doing us all a great favor). I beg to differ about what might seem to be a quibble. But the protest reveals, in any case, the same conclusion. That is, the state in a fully capitalist society does not assume that any function, beyond strictly legislative and judicial ones, is *uniquely appropriate* to it if the function is at all burdensome—not even the punishment and rehabilitation of those who have broken laws passed by legislature and have been judged by the judiciary.

What all this means is that corporate economic power will be the largest political power, because the state will be in a real sense subservient to it. Not just dependent on it (taxes). Not an equal partner with it (corporatism nominal or effective). No. *Subservient*—insidiously gripped by a muted assumption no sane person questions. Specifically: the assumption that there are no functions (legislative and judicial apparently aside) which are uniquely appropriate to the public sector, and that, finally, there is no such thing as *the uniquely appropriate.*

If you have a society in which there are no functions (the two exceptions still holding for the moment) which are thought to be beyond question appropriate to the public sector but not to the private, you also have a society in which traditions have no safety or respected legitimacy. Take one dramatic instance for speculative example: the precious idea that the profession of arms is a public function and that private armies are a danger to the *res publica.* I daresay it is not a judgment of "appropriateness" that forestalls the organization and capitalization of a National Protection Inc. to relieve the state of a burden so much as it is the fact that organizing and running the Inc. does not promise the sort of sure profits that private corrections corporations and such do. (But as I think "Blackwater," I wonder at that sentence.)

The history of this particular tradition, the public profession of arms (descendent of Plato's Guards), raises a pertinent point. When one talks about "the appropriate," one isn't necessarily talking about what has always been: were that the case, the discipline of history would be the study of utopia. The tradition of a public military is a relatively new and hard-won tradition, for sovereign states relied upon *condottieri* before the modern era as often or more than they relied upon conscript or standing armies. Yet, we think of it nonetheless as a public custom, and we're right to do so. The appropriate is not something to look for in "what's always been;" it's something to be discovered by intelligent moral consideration. Among those traditions long in place, that of public sector responsibility for judicial functions is safe enough. Although the encroachment upon its twin function—corrections—might give one pause, as well as might the hairy thought that some clever entrepreneurial J.D. is sitting up tonight thinking about backlogged dockets. It's safe enough because it's prescribed by the Constitution. As is, thank God, the legislature. But in the latter case . . . you don't have to privatize the legislative functions, so long as the assembly itself is gripped by your idea which has become a muted assumption.

The point is that even the honored tradition of republican government itself ceases to be a respected tradition with the degeneration of the idea that there are *functions uniquely appropriate to it*, never to be disowned or compromised by it, whether burdensome or light. Government in such an environment is capable of becoming a sort of residue of historical inertia. It would exist because it has existed. Representatives would legislate because they always have. There would be something to legislate about because, after all, there has to be something or other: the privatization of more of the state's responsibilities, for instance. Such leaden, passive isness is the last thing a tradition is. Tradition is what arises and survives because it is deeply felt to be necessary, appropriate. Otherwise, what is called tradition is only inertial convention.

The communist prejudice against "bourgeois parliamentary hypocrisy" could be dismissed. But government in a fully capitalist society is fully capable of giving that worn phrase some meaning through the active or passive compromise of *the concept of the uniquely appropriate*. The Jeffersonian dream "that government governs best which governs least" can come to mean "which governs hardly at all." Of course, there is a name for the bias that there are no functions legitimately and uniquely appropriate for the state. It's anarchism. Who could have predicted a century ago that anarchism would die or suffer senility as a communal doctrine, only to be reborn or rejuvenated as an extreme *laissez-faire* doctrine, "anarcho-capitalism?" That the Libertarian Party is now the third largest in the States may not be so relevant, electorally, given the intractability of two-party politics. But often groups, safely unburdened by official power, can articulate the deep logic of some in power, and so are not without significance in the broader scheme of ideas. The only thing that keeps libertarian ideology from preaching what Thomas Carlyle called "anarchy plus a constable" is that libertarians aren't sure about a *public* constabulary. Utopia is not only a no-place, it's a no-time. As the curmudgeonly Rebecca West (amazing how relevant she remains) once observed, "Anarchy is the most hopeless of faiths, being an aching discontent with time, which inexorably engenders order." The question is always "whose order?" That of those who believe in the uniquely appropriate or that of those who do not?

Let me repeat, and sum up provisionally, the point. What uniquely characterizes capitalism as a public philosophy is that muted assumption that there is no task uniquely appropriate to the public sector if it's potentially profitable to the private sector—and that, ultimately, there is no such thing as *the uniquely appropriate*. Furthermore and consequently, in a society governed by that assumption, there will be no ingrained, certainly no sustained, respect for tradition, since without the notion of the uniquely appropriate, there is no such thing as tradition, only inertial convention. Even representative assembly lives only as convention, existing through habit, lucky, in effect, that there are some tasks the private sector has yet to find potentially profitable.

How can conservatives spend so much mental passion in defense of a system and a public philosophy which hardly appear very conservative? American conservatives specifically, since it is American capitalism I'm talking about. Well, they can do it both or either because capitalism obviously works or in fear of socialism. Or because capitalism is the social institution that most matters because one is a Put-Con. And the motive need not be self-interest: a materialist explanation will not do, I don't think. For most of capitalism's conservative loyalists, even the Put-Cons, are not capitalists themselves. And for every hotshot policy intellectual rewarded with a comfortable think-tank birth, there are thousands of obscure editorial writers and college professors with patched herringbones and sensible 2000 Volvos with lumpy seats. Those I know well; they are some of my best friends (no Put-Cons included), most are rigorously intellectually honest—which is not the same thing as consistent. And I will assume the think-tankers are too. When I think of conservative friends and acquaintances, and if I think them representative, I cannot make do with an answer I know would be just in reference to Put-Cons, and in many cases among conservatives who are capitalists: not all American "conservatives" are conservative.

My friends are at least conservative enough to wish to support their apologetics with what strikes them as authentically conservative ammunition. But often, thereby they put themselves in an unexpected conundrum. Some of them, Catholic and otherwise, find a rich tradition in Catholic social doctrine, which they read with extraordinary selectivity and creativity. Any appeal to Catholic social teaching will begin with an appeal to St. Thomas Aquinas, to Aquinas' teaching, for instance that *private property* is a right protected by natural law—this in spite of the fact that the teaching *does not exist*. Rather, although private property is not against natural law, neither is it dictated by natural law: "the distribution of property is a matter not for natural law but, rather, human agreement, which is what positive law is all about" (*Summa Theologica*, 2a 2ae, 66). Or, there is the "principle of subsidiarity," for instance, to which the apologist might turn, which holds that what is no danger to the commonweal should be left to the exercise of private responsibility. But the apologist tends to ignore the fact that the other side of the principle of subsidiarity is that what is dangerous when left to private responsibility must not be left so. Enterprises which "carry with them power too great to be left in private hands, without injury to the community at large," as Pius XI put it in *Quadragesimo Anno*, which fact obviates the necessity of turning to *Mater et Magistra* of John XXIII where he'd find the same thing. The principle of subsidiarity, it should be observed, tacitly recognizes the notion of the uniquely appropriate.

I have yet to meet and know for some time a literate conservative who does not at some point mention or respond enthusiastically (along with me) to any mention of Richard Weaver's *Ideas Have Consequences* (1948), which has achieved the status of a kind of conservative holy writ—or a kind of *apocrypha* at least, the next best thing. The specific consequential idea from which began our "fearful descent" (Weaver's preferred title) into malaise, superficiality, violation of tradition was the medieval controversy over "Realism" vs. "Nominalism" and the triumph of the latter. A brave proposition, argued with passionate brilliance. Realism: the notion that universals (like the Platonic Idea or Form, as a matter of fact) have reality independent of our minds. Nominalism: the notion that universals are mere words, names, and abstractions with no independence from mind. From William of Occam through Francis Bacon and other circuits to modern positivism, the Nominalist "heresy" (so to say) has freed us of transcendent universal truths and left us to our own anarchic devices. I don't present this as an adequate summary of a subtle thesis. I only wish to hang upon Weaver's Realism a moment in order to make some connections.

I doubt that many of us spend much time in closeted speculation on medieval controversies, but I'm sure if you push a conservative to decision, he will line up passionately with Weaver on the Realist side. His habitual talk about liberal relativism, decline of standards, disrespect for fundamentals, loss of home truths, infatuations with the permissive, and so on, tell one as much. Such reflexes are the casual approximation of a metaphysical faith, a faith the conservative knows, just knows, must somehow be his. I know no other way to explain the status

Weaver's book enjoys in conservative circles—"the *fons et origo* of the contemporary American conservative movement" the late Frank Meyer judged—than the conservative's assumption that Weaver's Realism is theirs against liberal Nominalism. But when Weaver gets to specific applications of his Realism, the story should get too uncomfortable for intelligent conservative celebration.

To speak of Realism in the medieval sense, to endorse faith in universal truths which are more than convenient names assigned to this or that by the practical mind, is to assume that there is a certain *proprietas* native to an idea which cannot be shifted around, moved, or reassigned at will. Or a certain *Eigentum* or *hisness* as Weaver says, hammering home his point in another context. Now, I am not pursuing a strictly metaphysical or epistemological line here; rather, I am pursuing a set of associations which I think ought to resonate for a Realist. Which is what, in fact, Weaver is doing in *Ideas Have Consequences*, for all the metaphysical armory. One association is probably already apparent: *proprietas*, property, propriety, the appropriate, belongingness. There are properties of things, certain proprieties appropriate to certain things, certain things properly belong with certain things. And these "genitives," so to speak, are not mere names to be altered at will. Oh, of course they can be altered—but that's a "nominalist" act, without truth, with only interested convenience.

I can imagine a capitalist apologist fairly well salivating as he reads (selectively) Weaver. For Weaver is so taken with the *Eigentum* or *proprietas* of things that in its socio-economic, physical translation, the act of owning, Weaver finds "the last metaphysical right." There is a moral dimension to property, that is, the owned and the owner belonging to one another, the owning and the being owned a profounder matter than the mere names of possessor and estate. But it should be noted, as the apologist does not note it, that Weaver was talking about a property that has nothing to do with United Conglomerates Inc. For Weaver was one the last of the Agrarians. "The moral solution is the distributive ownership of small properties" in the "form of independent farms, of local businesses, of homes owned by the occupants, where individual responsibility gives significance to prerogative over property."

At this point, the apologist may raise his eyes from the page, smile with satisfaction, and reflect: so much greater then must be the significance of prerogative over really big property! But, "Such ownership," Weaver continues (referring to "small properties" and not reading his reader's mind) "provides a range of volition through which one can be a complete person, and it is the abridgement of this volition for which monopoly capitalism must be condemned along with communism." The apologist blanches for a moment, fixes for a minute on "monopoly" instead of "capitalism," is briefly disturbed by the suggestion that communism and capitalism are "morally equivalent" as one would say today, and then forgets.

I am not trying to suggest what Weaver's idea of the specific unique properties of the public sector were; I'm only suggesting that Weaver's perspective must have it that there have to be certain functions uniquely appropriate to government, as there are functions uniquely appropriate to any human realm, not to be shifted about, moved, or reassigned at "nominalist" will. Weaver's is not a perspective the Put-Con ought to be comfortable with: since the notion of "unique property" is not one of the Put-Con's muted assumptions, all the phrase could mean to him is a singular piece of real estate.

What the apologist ever saw in Weaver would be beyond me were it not clear that he could read selectively, could after a brief genuflection ignore the reflections on *proprietas* as an irrelevant Latinate professorial flight, and pretend that Weaver's animadversions in the passage quoted above were directed at those few bad capitalists (any barrel has its rotten fruit), while Weaver clearly meant the ideological barrel itself was the problem. But nonetheless and nevertheless, Weaver helped them along:

Considering the abridgement of volition for which capitalism as well as communism must be held responsible, a result would seem to be suggested by Weaver's image of "the besotted middle class, grown enormous under the new orientation of

Western man." This class, "having comfort, risking little, terrified at the thought of change," aims only to "banish threats to its complacency. It has conventions, not ideals; it is washed rather than clean." A description of bourgeoisie under capitalism? No. Or somehow no more than incidentally if at all. Rather: a characterization of middle class under socialist ideals, which somehow or other Weaver imagines reigning. "It clarifies much to see that socialism is in origin a middle-class and not a proletarian concept." Historically, of course, that's true, as of practically any –ism, which is totally irrelevant to the point. "Socialism" here is a euphemism for communism? No. It is "social democracy" that Weaver imagines Americans to be living under in 1948—which was true only to the degree that some New Deal programs still survived. Surely Weaver was exaggerating, but this was not merely Weaver's singular fancy, for it's something like a reflex he shares with many conservatives who are more sympathetic to capitalism than he was.

It seems to be a unique property of pro-capitalist polemic to talk half the time as if capitalism doesn't exist. Perhaps it does during periods of Reaganite ascendancy, but during periods of liberal ascendancy, even before the time of the rockstar presidency and the Obamanoids, capitalism was fighting a gallant battle for its own rebirth against an essentially socialist D.C.; then it's socialism that exists (creeping at the least). I don't know why Weaver was subject to this public derangement, since he had no fondness for capitalism in the first place, only an animosity toward the socialism he cast off at the feet of the Agrarian John Crowe Ransom. But I think I know why so many capitalist apologists, and certainly the Put-Cons, are subject to the derangement.

Capitalism is no respecter of the transcendent truths, the universals, which a "Realist" faith implies. And occasionally an apologist will admit as much, as when Michael Novak noted several years ago, "Democratic capitalism undermines all traditions and institutions (even itself)." The parenthetical "even itself" I take to be a kind of spirited humor, as if to say that capitalism is in a state of permanent revolution through which it looks a little different every decade or so but survives intact in all essentials. Anyone who admires such macho upheavals in the *Zeitgeist* is going to turn to Weaver's high-minded Latinity of thought only when he needs a bit of elegant mental entertainment, wishes a little classiness to rub off; but it won't mean much more than that: it can't. What does have meaning is the incompleteness of the upheaval. That is, capitalism may "undermine," but the problem is that the undermining has not been completed. So voracious is the appetite for completion that without it, capitalism is often perceived to be not really here yet. But—one might ask as one reads the papers, peruses *Business Week*, follows administrations, and in general merely observes the world one lives in—how is capitalism not completed. I think the answer is the following.

There remains the essentially Platonic notion, no matter how differently stated and no matter how imperfectly embraced, that there are some things which are uniquely appropriate to the public sector. I don't think the notion is consciously held by many people, except as a kind of inertial residue. At least I cannot imagine many people intoning, "functions uniquely appropriate, never to be disowned or compromised, whether burdensome or light," etc. But however weak the notion, its merest existence is an affront to the capitalist spirit, which cannot be at ease with the thought that anything could resist its embraces. So long as all human institutional functions have not been privatized, capitalism's enthusiasts will periodically behave as if capitalism is only a brave hope for the future instead of the central present fact of our socio-economic existence.

Will *periodically* behave so. To sustain the illusion—or pretense—at all times would be too demanding. At other moments, the apologists may face with some equanimity the fact that some functions are at present withheld from the private sector. But what is always offensive is the merest thought that somebody thinks that those functions *should* be withheld because of their nature, because they would be inappropriate (not just at present unprofitable) to the private sector. That thought is so offensive because it is resistant to the idea becoming a muted assumption which makes capitalism *really* capital-*ism*, not markets and capital formation, necessary to any sophisticated economy, but the implicit dismissal of the Platonic notion of the *uniquely appropriate*.

So, Plato does indeed remain *relevant*—relevant, that is, if one is seeking the truth. Unfortunately, however, relevant does not translate as *influential*. It is difficult-to-impossible for me to imagine the Put-Con enthusiast for unbridled capitalism, impatient with any incursions from the public realm, so much as reading a page of Plato (unless having had *The Apology* forced upon him in some required—and now forgotten—survey). But the Put-Con apologist himself remains *intellectually ir-relevant*.

Back when I was a socialist, I was not right that socialism is the better conserver of "the permanent things"—but I was not altogether wrong, I am not wrong that a reverent attitude toward capitalism is not a natural component of conservatism alone. Capitalism is, in spite of its often revolutionary volatility, finally consistent with a conservative disposition, but is not a necessary part of its definition. In the words of one of Irving Kristol's early titles: *Two Cheers for Capitalism*, not three.

WHAT MOTIVATED NIETZSCHE?

KENNETH FRANCIS

THE YEAR 2020 WAS the beginning of an Orwellian night-mare in the twenty-first century, with the lockdown restrictions on human freedom. Near the end of the nineteenth century, philosopher Friedrich Nietzsche advocated—and partially succeeded—tearing down the Old Normal to create a New Normal called the Transvaluation of all Values. A similar thing is happening all over again today, but with greater power, velocity and tyranny, with Christianity being the most persecuted religion in the world.[1] As the old idiom states: History repeats itself.

---

1 ACN research, *Christian Persecution: The Persecution of Christians is on the Rise Worldwide, Aid to the Church in Need*, https://www.churchinneed.org/christian-persecution/.

As for Friedrich Nietzsche (1844-1900), the problem with writing about famous historical figures is revealing fresh biographical material about them. For example, spare a thought for the hagiographers for the next books on St. Paul or Pontius Pilate. There's not much else to be known about them that hasn't already been written. The same applies to Friedrich Nietzsche, who famously proclaimed: "God is dead."

Maybe sometime in the not-too-distant future a box of unread letters penned by him might be discovered, but it's unlikely such a treasure trove will be found. And even if a discovery were made, one would rightly question the authenticity of such a find or whether the material had been expurgated for propaganda purposes.

What I can offer are some reflections on what might have motivated Nietzsche's bleak worldview. We can assume he was a protégé of the great pessimist and a highly influential thinker of 19th century philosophy, Arthur Schopenhauer (1778-1860). But before examining the motives behind Nietzsche's chaotic philosophy, let me briefly comment on the possible motivations of other so-called "visionaries," possibly inspired by Nietzsche, whose works had, and still have, a negative impact on Western Christian civilisation, or what's left of it. I'm talking about the metaphorical "Four Horsemen" of the Western Culture apocalypse: Relativism, Modernism, Postmodernism and Nihilism.

I sometimes look at Brutalist architecture and wonder whether the architect was psychologically abused as a child. I think to myself: "Whoever constructed this deformed monstrosity badly needed to see a psychiatrist." I'm sure there are many sane wonderful people who design Brutalist architecture, but some of the giant blocks ruining many cityscapes make me wonder if their designers were, or are, insane. There's something quite aggressively sick about such monolithic structures in the metropolis archipelago of the Western world.

I've no doubt that if Le Corbusier were alive today, he'd be part of the same city planning gang designing "smart cities" that would repel the human soul with public squares turned into airport-style glass gargantuan structures of surveillance hell and spatial anomie.

In our visual and spiritual existence, the soul seeks harmony while the brain seeks patterns, none of which exist in these crushing Brutalist giant blocks of the downtown concrete jungles of the West and beyond. One wonders, did "progressive" architects seek revenge on mankind by vandalizing cities with such hideous structures? Or did Nietzsche's nihilism have a part to play by consciously or unconsciously influencing the minds of city planners, architects and artists?

What kind of warped construction in the deep recesses of the mind can destroy the classic harmony of a street of beautiful Georgian houses and replace them with a series of giant, ugly concrete blocks? Perhaps a Nietzschean mind with a Dionysian mentality that doesn't correspond to the natural order of perceiving objective traditional beauty, or the minds of aesthetic relativists who would say "beauty is subjective" might find those buildings pleasing.

Is a banana held to a wall by duct tape in an "art" gallery[2] more beautiful than *The Creation of Adam*[3] fresco painting on the Sistine Chapel ceiling? Or, the bland Royal Liverpool Hospital building compared to the architecture of the beautiful University of Oxford? As Theodore Dalrymple has written:

> Certainly, brutalism is to architecture what American pit bulls are to dogs, that is to say ugly, menacing and aggressive. Recently, there has been a concerted attempt, almost a propagandistic campaign, to persuade us that these concrete blockhouses are not merely innovative (that they were, alas!) but beautiful.

> There is a curious thing about the glossy photographs of brutalist buildings that are published in a spate of expensive books intended to persuade us that our initial reaction of horror is wrong: they are entirely abstract in the sense that no human figure is allowed to sully them, indeed there is nothing

---

2 Maurizio Cattelan, *Comedian*, Instalment of Art Basel Miami Beach, 2019.

3 Michelangelo, *The Creation of Adam*, Sistine Chapel, Rome, circa 1508-1512.

with any possible reference to humanity in them that could spoil the geometry of the conception behind the buildings, as if architecture were merely a three-dimensional Mondrian painting rather than a built space in which human beings made their lives, or some part of their lives. The buildings are portrayed as vast empty tombs, but without the grandeur (or archaeological interest) of the Pyramids.[4]

But, as mentioned above, it's not just buildings that are subjected to "architectural terrorism." The same applies to some specimens of Modern "Art" installations, which can have a profound inaesthetic effect on our conscious well-being and concept of humanity. There are lots of examples of what passes for art, but instead such works in Brutalist galleries and public squares disconnect our soul from their visual effects, which brings me back to psychological motivations.

Could being scolded for not making your bed as a child, or some other life-trauma event, manifest in an infamous installation at London's Tate Gallery,[5] which later sold for £2.5m? Or, could punishment for early bed-wetting result in a signed Fountain porcelain urinal at a prestigious French museum of modern and contemporary art?[6]

And, was a young Andy Warhol force-fed Campbell's soup before going to school every morning?[7] Or, was Samuel Beckett regularly stood-up by his best friend (probably called Godfrey) and left waiting with another buddy during his boyhood years?[8] Perhaps we'll never know. It's only a matter of time when the Turner Prize will go to a stained medical face-mask floating in a tank of formaldehyde at The Tate. Such a piece might even be entitled: *Face Nappies a-Floatin' After the Lockdown.*

But why would someone bestow such ugliness on a potential spectator seeking beauty in the arts? Admittedly, for some

---

4 Theodore Dalrymple, "Brutalism," *New English Review*, January 2021.

5 Tracey Emin, *My Bed*, 1998; at Tate Gallery, 1999.

6 Marcel Duchamp, *Fountain*, 1917, Modern Art Museum, Nice, France.

7 Andy Warhol, *Campbell's Soup Cans*, 1961.

8 Samuel Beckett, *Waiting for Godot*, 1953.

people, these obscure objects of un-desire can sometimes look intriguing in a Theatre-of-the-Absurdesque way. This also occurred to me in the writings of some of the world's most "progressive" philosophers, novelists and composers who seemed to have rationalised and justified their own degenerate worldview under the guise of Modernism, the sister worldview of Postmoderism and Relativism.

Consider elements of alleged licentious revenge in the works of Wagner (*Tristan und Isolde*), Freud and Kinsey (Sexual Revolution), Marx and Nietzsche (nihilistic anti-Christianity), and the atonal "music" of Schoenberg. There is something bitter brewing in the psychology of all of the above-named icons.

Was Nietzsche's godless world view formed on the psychological basis of the death of his father, when little Friedrich was aged four, thus his desire to mentally replace the father-figure god-shaped hole in the form of a superman[9] deity?

Like Schopenhauer, the powerful, poetic, emotional rhythm of Nietzsche's prose is of a literary quality reminiscent of biblical chapter and verse, which probably, paradoxically, inspired the infamous anti-Christian who regularly read the Bible; and, unlike the stiff and awkward rambling scribbles of other philosophers, who probably spent too much time in academia, many famous 20th century writers have paid homage to Schopenhauer and Nietzsche's prose as great inspirations for literary device.

But despite the terrible beauty of Nietzsche's texts, darkness prevails, as death or despair without hope constantly raises its ugly head. Which brings us back again to the passing of Nietzsche's father.

During a 2014 talk in America on Nietzsche, hosted by the Franciscan University, the psychologist Paul Vitz said many of the German philosopher's biographers have pointed out that Nietzsche never got over the death of his father, whom he deeply loved. Dr Vitz said that in many ways, his search for a father was expressed in his idealisation of a search for the "su-

---

9 Friedrich Nietzsche, "Ubermensch," "Beyond Man," *Thus Spoke Zarathustra*, 1883.

perman."[10]

Speculation on the psychological matters for the formation of one's character is endless. One could even wonder whether Nietzsche's mother was badly beaten with a stick by a mad nun while she was pregnant with little foetus Freddie. And, as mentioned, the same can be speculated for many of his contemporaries.

The hostility the godless German philosopher had for Christianity was on a par with those who condemned Jesus to death by crucifixion. However, in fairness to him, no one can accuse Nietzsche of not having the courage to challenge his own godless conviction and the ramifications of "murdering" God.

In "The Parable of the Madman,"[11] it's obvious Nietzsche assumes the persona of the tragic mad character who enters the marketplace to tell the godless crowds the consequences of their actions in killing the Creator of the Universe. With the aid of emotive metaphor, infused with bleak, nightmarish eloquent rhetoric, the Madman asks the crowd: "Who gave us the sponge to wipe away the entire horizon? What were we doing when we unchained this earth from its sun?"

The reader of this spectacular prose finds his mind spun into a whirlwind of existential vertigo, as the Madman evokes humanity straying into the darkest of all nights; a world of infinite nothing, where we breathe empty space and everything is getting colder and bleaker; a world where we're plunging continually, backward, sideward, and forward, not knowing if there is any up or down, as we smell the divine decomposition as the gravediggers bury God whom we have murdered: The murderers of all murders!

And Nietzsche's right. But he's wrong to think we can overcome this and improve our destiny. Without God, the self no longer exists, as humans become a multitude of mature germs evolved into hairless apes roaming planet Earth at the mercy

---

10 Franciscan University Presents: *Faith of the Fatherless: The Psychology of Atheism*; November 11, 2014; https://www.youtube.com.

11 Friedrich Nietzsche, "Parable of the Madman," *The Gay Science* (1882, 1887).

of physics, chemistry and environment—a sea of meaningless molecules swirling in empty space.

For anyone who truly understands the meaning of logic or reason, Jesus Christ was/is the Logos, the Truth incarnate. But ever since Nietzsche and the modern world, objective Truth has become beyond the scope of "respectable" conversation or debate in Woke anti-Logos circles where feelings of sexual degenerate "liberation" and emotions prevail.

Consider what Nietzsche wrote in *The Antichrist*: "I call Christianity the one great curse, the one great intrinsic depravity, the one great instinct for revenge for which no expedient (i.e. A means of attaining an end, especially one that is convenient but considered improper or immoral) is sufficiently poisonous, secret, subterranean, petty —I call it the one immortal blemish of mankind... And one calculates time from the *dies nefastus* on which this fatality arose—from the 'first' day of Christianity! Why not rather from its last? From today? Revaluation of all values!"[12]

This destructive declaration gave great comfort to theologically illiterate psychopathic world leaders, as well as sex-degenerates seeking moral autonomy. For if God does not exist, then objective moral values and duties do not exist, thus everything is amoral, neither objectively right nor wrong. To phrase it another way: "Shit happens." It means the universe is just a brute fact, and the creatures which inhabit the earth are nothing more than atoms in motion. And it's not a sin to squash an atom.

But let us examine if Nietzsche's bleak words are right or wrong. Without God, we would be nothing more than advanced, overgrown germs, blindly fighting for survival of the fittest. For Social Justice Warriors and Woke virtue-signallers of the world, think about the implications of this the next time you scream "Racist!" "Homophobe!" "Bigot!" "Nazi!" or otherwise express an unjustified hatred for your fellow human beings. This would be nothing more than the situational movements of molecular puppets without freedom of the will. And if this be the case,

---

12 Nietzsche, Conclusion, *The Antichrist* (1895), Cosimo ed, 2005, ISBN 978-1-59605-681-7.

then why did Nietzsche assume we could break free from religion and become superhuman? How can a creature, whose fate is determined by the forces of nature, free his or herself from the "chains of religion?" How could Nietzsche freely choose to raise his wrist and proclaim God is dead? Can an oak tree refuse to grow branches? Can grass refuse to grow over two inches tall?

But in Nietzsche's world, such sad accidental creatures would be encouraged to one day strive to become supermen (a tall task for the advanced, hairless chimp).

Whatever it was that motivated Nietzsche, one thing is certain: The legacy of this self-appointed anti-Christ is negative. He not only scorned reason, but his views had some impact on the religious persecution against Christians worldwide, as well as anarchy on the streets of US cities and the bloodbath that was the twentieth-century under Communism, with over 100 million innocent people slaughtered or starved to death.

The author, Dr. Alex Chediak, wrote: "Man is incurably religious. We were made to worship the Triune God and to live in a state of unbroken fellowship with our God. In this world, we have an innate sense of exile, of disconnectedness, of brokenness. We're not in our true home yet. Experiences of beauty in music, art or nature often awaken in us a sense of longing, a desire to follow the beauty as it were, back to its Source. C.S. Lewis and others have discussed how this longing bears testimony to our spiritual nature, to our being made to enjoy God."[13]

The elite might not be classical Nietzscheans, but they will surely cherry-pick the core message that emanates from the death of God and the many evil idols on offer in a world without justice.

Even the atheist philosopher Bertrand Russell acknowledged that a world without God will not help us to come to terms with the existence of evil and our passion for justice. Russell wrote about man being the product of causes that had no prevision of the end they were achieving. That his origin, his growth, his hopes and fears, his loves, his beliefs are but the

---

13 Alex Chediak, *The Stream* (online blog), October 29, 2020, https://stream. org/are-we-living-in-a-video-game/.

outcome of accidental collocations of atoms.[14]

In conclusion: Nietzsche died insane in bed, on August 25, 1900. Be very, very careful in following his ideas of burying God and declaring the Creator dead. Accidental atoms have no concern for Truth, Justice or Reason. And in these dark days of lockdowns, if a rogue snitcher-neighbour hears you sneezing in bed, a SWAT team of atoms might knock on your door at midnight and forcibly take you away to a concentration camp—I mean, quarantine center—allegedly for your own safety and the safety of other atoms. Such blind motivations for the atoms' tyranny will only be falling in line with Nietzsche's Transvaluations of values where might is right and the means are justified by the ends.

---

14 Bertrand Russell, "A Free Man's Worship," in *Mysticism and Logic and Other Essays* (London: Allen & Unwin, 1963).